"Don't be a fool!"

BY MICHAEL GERBER

TRIGGER WARNING

Dr. Strangelove is great...but maybe it's time for Inspector Clouseau?

I'm writing this in mid-October, assuming that Donald Trump has lost. If not, please send any faux-outraged responses or coded messages to: Inmate 57631, Camp Ultimate Freedom, Tebbets, MO 65080.)

I have, like all of you, spent this entire election cycle slowly throwing up. But then I remembered all the things I learned in college. Like how in the run-up to the Lincoln/Douglas debates, Abe bragged about "brazenly tweaking Joshua Speed's man-carrot." Or how Dwight Eisenhower confided to a *Stars and Stripes* reporter that he only wanted to be President "to finger-bang visiting dignitaries." Or how Nixon called Jews an "irreligious, atheistic, immoral bunch of bastards."

Of course Nixon actually said that, but that was Nixon, a man made entirely of beard stubble and wet garbage. And next to Donald Trump, Richard Nixon looks like freaking Pericles.

Let's not kid ourselves: This was what NASA calls "a near-miss." What we escaped exactly, we don't know, but it would have been no birthday party. Unless you consider mass deportations,

MICHAEL GERBER

(@mgerber937) is the Chairman of *The American Bystander*.

free-range sexual assault, and a nuclear exchange with China, a proper way to celebrate your 40th.[1]

Trump was a zesty blend of all of the most odious aspects of American politics, and it should be the goal of every citizen to make sure nothing like him ever happens again. This is so obvious, why am I typing it at you? Because I think comedy has something to do with how we got here.

First of all — and this is where I'll lose people, in addition to all the Nixon apologists who've already left — I believe there's altogether too much satire going on these days. Yes, yes, we're living in a Golden Age, which I enjoy along with the rest of you — but satire is to politics what pornography is to sex: harmless in the right amount, but bad news when it becomes a steady diet. Its fear- and anger-based exaggeration creates exactly the wrong mindset for responsible democracy. Satire heats up the blood. Yes, there can be a benefit to moving people to action — but hundreds of exposures a day via Twitter or Facebook, and you run a real risk that you're no longer living in reality.

Trump is the product of an overheated, hysterical society. But whereas Weimar Germany (to pick an example at random) was lashed by almost unimaginable economic and societal trauma — World War I, the flu, hyperinflation,

[1] Heads up, it's not. My wife's still pissed.

private armies fighting in the streets — *nothing like that is happening here.* Most people are safe. Most people have a job. Most people have enough to eat. Trump supporters are not African-Americans rightly angry at cops shooting kids. They aren't even debt-crushed millennials plumping for a *Götterdämmerung* reset. They are, too many of them, rank-and-file Republicans, people for whom this society works.

Unlike Weimar, this crisis isn't happening in the real world; it's happening in people's minds. And this is where comedy comes in — or more precisely, satire.

Comedy, like everything else, is cyclical, swinging between realistic and imaginative at regular intervals. Our current, realistic, cycle began in 1999, when Jon Stewart reimagined *The Daily Show*. And thank God he did; how would we have gotten through 9/11 and the Bush years without Stewart, Colbert, and *The Onion*? This legacy is being carried on admirably by John Oliver and Samantha Bee, and maybe even you. Thanks to Facebook and Twitter, satire is perhaps our national pastime.

At the same time, our national conversation has continued to decay, and I think I see why. As the mainstream has turned to satire for its news, the fringes have grown alarmed. The fringes don't get irony; they only hear the exaggeration. So they react *as if the satire is serious*, getting more and more paranoid and feeling more and more under attack. They think, for example, Obama's coming for their guns — when in fact there are more guns than ever (twice as many per capita than in 1968).

The mainstream is laughing, but we're frightened too; great satire carries terror just under the laughter. Now social media allows you to binge, to live in satire in a way that wasn't possible before, and most people's nervous systems can't take it. TL;DR — America is way too terrified to have a sensible conversation about anything.

But wait, there's more: as satire has become our *lingua franca*, politicians have increasingly co-opted satire's techniques without accepting its responsibilities. Over and over, Donald Trump acted as if he were performing, as if he were the alt-Right's own George Carlin speaking truth to power. "Locker-room talk." "Sarcasm." "Entertainment." Over and over, Trump — a fact-free plutocrat without a speck of civic feeling — claimed the indulgence of truth-telling shaman-satirist.

But St. Lenny didn't die for The Donald's sins; just because something offends, that doesn't make it a *joke*. Intent means everything. The more outrageous satire is, the more it requires discipline, and decency. And reading comprehension; the alt-Right strikes me as a bunch of white men who read *A Modest Proposal* and came away thinking baby-eating was a great idea. As dark, exaggerated, ironic satire has become more and more of our national conversation, more and more people aren't getting the joke.

So what do we, the comedy-friendly non-insane, do about this? I think we need more silly. For one thing, silly is harmless; it will reduce the temperature. For another, comedy needs to go somewhere authority figures can't follow. When the CIA's cracking wise on its Twitter feed, something's broken, and more satire won't fix it.

In times dominated by reality-based comedy, the imaginative type often feels lesser, but it's no small thing to entertain. And when exquisite satire is surrounded by silliness (see: *Brian, Life of*) it packs an incredible wallop. Finally, silly lasts — nobody reads Will Rogers anymore, but we still watch the Marx Brothers.

We want *Bystander* to be a respite, a refuge — so much so that I really considered not mentioning the election at all; but that seemed perverse in its own way. Still, we won't make a habit of it. Daily news churn, plus corporate comedy, plus social media will throw up satire from now until the Sun explodes. And in its proper place, that's a fine thing and a fun thing but not *our* thing. We go a different way, not to ignore what's happening but to heal it.

I don't have the answer. I only have a strong suspicion that contemporary satire — angry, dark, hyperbolic and omnipresent — played a role in creating Donald Trump, Almost President. The canary in our coal mine isn't dead, but it has passed out. Care to join us in a little mouth-to-beak?

············ ◆ ············

P.S. *Thing one:* There is a growing tide of loose talk involving a UK-based version of *Bystander*, to provide an outlet for all the wonderful writers and artists skulking in and around Albion. Of course, we need 3,000 backers for this to happen. Watch this space.

Thing two: Fearless Leader Brian asks me after every issue, "Are people writing us?" Now normally, I advocate ignoring the comments section of pretty much everything for reasons of simple mental health. But *Bystander* readers are worlds away from the usual cyber-droogs, so I am theoretically amenable to running missives from you all. Interesting facts, gripping reports, honest expressions of befuddlement, reports on the ground — all of these and more are welcome. If we get anything publishable, well, we'll publish it.

I've set up an email address: *Letters@ americanbystander.org*. Get cracking. Until then: Take a breath. Relax. Laugh. And enjoy the issue. **B**

TABLE OF CONTENTS

Whole No. 3 • Fall 2016 • americanbystander.org

DIANE BALDWIN

DEPARTMENTS

Frontispiece: "Don't Be A Fool!" *by Gahan Wilson*................. 1
Publisher's Letter *by Michael Gerber* 2
News and Notes..9
Classifieds 86
Index to This Issue *by The Pleasure Syndicate* 89
Crossword #2: "Brush Up Your Insults"
   by Matt Matera & Alan Goldberg.......................................92

GALLIMAUFRY

Al Jean, Michael Weithorn, Megan Koester, John Howell Harris, P.S. Mueller, Steve Young, Dave Hanson, Lee Sachs, Broti Gupta, Dirk Voetberg, Zack Bornstein, Katie Schwartz, R.D. Rosen, Brian McConnachie, Jocelyn Richard, and Jack Handey.

SHORT STUFF

Nobody Dies, They Just Get Bigger *by M.K. Brown*...................5
The Park *by Billy Collins, illustrated by George Booth* 7
Ali Is Still Champ *by Ted Jouflas* 12
Pick Up Artistry *by Hana Michels*...........................25
Who Am I? *by Brian McConnachie* 26
Star Wars Script Meeting *by Steve Young* 28
Everything Has A Problem *by Quentin Hardy*...................31
What Am I Doing Here? *by Mike Reiss* 32
It's Getting Hard to Find a Good Henchman These Days
   by P.S. Mueller 34
How To Get Along With Friends and Relatives Stupid Enough
  to Be Voting for the Wrong Side *by Merrill Markoe* 36
Love and Mercy 2 *by J.A. Weinstein* 63
A Letter to the Commish *by Brian McConnachie* 64
The Tree of Shitty Wisdom *by Ben Orlin*......................66
My Dinner With Ennui *by Michael Thornton* 68
About Our "C" *by Jay Ruttenberg* 70

FEATURES

The Ballad of Three-Bean Salad *by Mike Reiss*........................38
Common Bodies Without Beauty *by Ron Barrett*.............40
Dirtbags *by Mallory Ortberg*................................44
Chapter One: *Downturn Abbey by Michael Gerber*...............48

The AMERICAN BYSTANDER

EDITOR & PUBLISHER
Michael Gerber
HEAD WRITER Brian McConnachie
SENIOR EDITOR Alan Goldberg
DEPUTY EDITORS
Michael Thornton, Ben Orlin

CONTRIBUTORS Diane Baldwin, Jeremy Banx, Ron Barrett, Charles Barsotti, Louisa Bertman, Chris Bonno, George Booth, Zack Bornstein, M.K. Brown, David Chelsea, Billy Collins, Howard Cruse, John Cuneo, Etienne Delessert, Nick Downes, Xeth Feinberg, Drew Friedman, Tom Gammill, Rick Geary, Sam Gross, Broti Gupta, Jack Handey, Dave Hanson, Quentin Hardy, John Howell Harris, Al Jean, Ted Jouflas, Megan Koester, Ken Krimstein, Peter Kuper, David Lancaster, Sara Lautman, Eugenia Loli, Merrill Markoe, Scott Marshall, Matt Matera, Michael Maslin, Hana Michels, P.S. Mueller, Joe Oesterle, Mallory Ortberg, Ethan Persoff, Mimi Pond, Jonathan Plotkin, Mike Reddy, Mike Reiss, Jocelyn Richard, R.D. Rosen, Jay Ruttenberg, Lee Sachs, Katie Schwartz, Cris Shapan, Michael Sloan, Grant Snider, Rich Sparks, Nick Spooner, The Pleasure Syndicate, Tom Toro, Dirk Voetberg, D. Watson, J.A. Weinstein, Michael Weithorn, Gahan Wilson, Steve Young, and Jack Ziegler.
COPYEDITING BY Chuck Ferrara
THANKS TO Rae Barsotti, Kate Powers, Karen Backus, Molly Bernstein, Joe Lopez, Eliot Ivanhoe, Neil Gumenick, Thomas Simon, and many others, including evangelists Christian Albrecht, Mike Barrow, Timothy Black, Darryl Byrne, King Cormack, and Tim Hulsizer.
NAMEPLATE BY Mark Simonson
ISSUE CREATED BY Michael Gerber

NOBODY DIES
THEY JUST GET BIGGER

I BELIEVE YOU KNOW MY PARENTS, FRED AND EDITH?

JEFFREY, PLEASE PASS YOUR GREAT-GREAT-GREAT-GREAT-GRANPA THE CROISSANTS.

THANK YOU, JEFFREY!

OH, LOOK! IT'S ELEANOR ROOSEVELT!

A MAY-DECEMBER WEDDING

HOLD IT RIGHT THERE, "JACK." YOU'RE UNDER ARREST, AT LAST.

WOULDN'T YOU KNOW—EVERY TIME YOU TRY TO HAVE A NICE TIME, ALONG COMES SOME DAMN ANCESTOR.

WHERE WILL IT ALL END?

Noah and the Dinosaurs *by Merrill Markoe* 54
The Worst Thing I Ever Did *by Rick Geary* 56
A Dance To Feiffer *by Peter Kuper* 57
A Rendez-Vous With *The New Yorker* *by Michael Maslin* 59

COMICS
The Diary of Merrill Markoe: Actual Excerpts
    by Merrill Markoe 73
Tales of the Quicksand Kid *by Howard Cruse* 74
John Wilcock: ECHO Magazine
    by Ethan Persoff and Scott Marshall 77
The Kids Movie *by David Chelsea* 79
Ironic Fashion Role Models *by Mimi Pond* 83
Zen of Nimbus *by Michael Sloan* 84
The Doozies *by Tom Gammill* 84

CARTOONS & ILLUSTRATIONS BY
Peter Arno, Diane Baldwin, Jeremy Banx, Charles Barsotti, Louisa Bertman, Chris Bonno, George Booth, M.K. Brown, David Chelsea, John Cuneo, Etienne Delessert, Nick Downes, Xeth Feinberg, Tom Gammill, Rick Geary, Sam Gross, Ted Jouflas, Ken Krimstein, Peter Kuper, David Lancaster, Sara Lautman, Eugenia Loli, Joe Oesterle, Jonathan Plotkin, Mike Reddy, Cris Shapan, Michael Sloan, Grant Snider, Rich Sparks, Nick Spooner, Tom Toro, D. Watson, Gahan Wilson, and Jack Ziegler.

COVER
"American Bystanders" by Drew Friedman.

"This is shit. We're going to publish it."

ACKNO WLEDG MENTS

All material in this issue of *The American Bystander* is ©2016 its creators, all rights reserved. It may not be reproduced or distributed by any means, electronic or otherwise, without the prior written consent of the creators and *The American Bystander*.

The following material has previously appeared, and is reprinted here with permission of the authors:

Mallory Ortberg's "Dirtbag MacBeth," "Dirtbag Athena," and "Dirtbag Teddy Roosevelt" appeared at The-Toast.com, which is just full of good stuff. If it's really out of business, we are heartbroken and don't care who knows it.

"He Said It!" (our title, in case you don't like it) first emerged on John Howell Harris' delightful Bartlettsfamiliarquotations.tumblr.com.

"Chapter One: *Downturn Abbey*," is excerpted from the book-length parody by Michael Gerber, published 2012 and reprinted courtesy of the author (duh). The full book is available on Amazon.com, B&N.com, and via special order at any bookstore.

Michael Sloan's "Memory Box: The Man With the Homburg Hat" is from michael-sloanillustration.tumblr.com. Michael's "Zen of Nimbus" graphic novels and assorted merch can be purchased via his website, zenofnimbus.com

"John Wilcock: The New York Years— ECHO Magazine" debuted at Boingboing.net. It later appeared in Persoff & Marshall's Wilcock collection. *John Wilcock: New York Years, 1954-1971* is available at Blurb.com and well worth whatever they're charging for it.

"A Rendez-Vous With *The New Yorker*" is excerpted from Michael Maslin's biography *Peter Arno: The Mad, Mad World of* The New Yorker's *Greatest Cartoonist*. It is reprinted here courtesy of the author and Knopf.

The Park

Just because a dog or a cat or even a hen
does not know how old it is
does not mean it is not that old.

Sometimes you can tell.

Like an ancient sparrow
making its way on crutches
past the fountain onto the grass.

And there's the white of the muzzle,
or a smaller dog favoring a forepaw
on its daily walk around the block.

But what about this crow
in its judicial robes
looking down from a branch
at the commotion of the park?

As timeless as he looks,
it could be his birthday
for all anyone knows.

No need for candles or cards,
he's only a black hole on a snowy day.

So many mornings
I must have walked below him
without even tipping my cap.

—Billy Collins

The *Charlie Hebdo* of American Satire

The Realist (1958-2001) was the legendary satirical magazine published by Paul Krassner —
provocateur, radical, yippie, prankster — that struck from below with humor and ridicule.
Outrageous cartoons were the highlight of each issue — some of the most incendiary ever to
appear in an American magazine.

The Realist Cartoons collects for the very first time the best drawings from the magazine's
historic run, including work by R. Crumb, Art Spiegelman, S. Clay Wilson, Jay Lynch, Wallace
Wood, Trina Robbins, Mort Gerberg, Jay Kinney, Wallace Wood, Trina Robbins, Richard
Guindon, Nicole Hollander, Skip Williamson, and many others.

"Paul Krassner is an activist, a philosopher, a lunatic and a saint, but most of all he is funny."
— Lewis Black

FANTAGRAPHICS BOOKS

WWW.FANTAGRAPHICS.COM

NEWS & NOTES

JOHN CUNEO

From the Be-Careful-What-You-Save Department: **HOWARD CRUSE**'s private archives were recently acquired by Columbia University's Rare Books and Manuscripts Library, which explains the derisive sniggering emanating from the darker reaches of the Butler Library by cataloguers just beginning to uncover embarrassing poetry he composed as a high schooler in Alabama. He is now at work on a memoir covering the many embarrassing things he has done in adulthood...**P.S. MUELLER** writes, "I have been hard at it with the matter of silly drawings and my latestest incarnation of Onion Audible News anchor Doyle Redland, which means I have become an app, freed of all human confinement." In addition to being all over this issue, our favorite app also has a story in *Rosebud Magazine*...**MIKE SACKS** opened for David Sedaris at two events this past fall, *not* fulfilling his childhood dream. His childhood dream was to become a brain surgeon, and then a pilot, and then a temp working at an office park off I-270 in suburban Maryland, next to a fake lake surrounded by a ton of geese shit...**J.A. WEINSTEIN** (@JohnnyStyne) publicly states: "I recently ferried to beautiful Hoboken, New Jersey, for an in-studio appearance on Artie Lange's *The ArtieQuitter Podcast* (ArtieQuitter. com) #297, in which I became the first *AQPC* guest to blatantly and shamelessly hawk *The American Bystander*." We hope he is not the last. J.A. is an NFL fan and, in addition to giving the Publisher fantasy advice, remains pathologically perturbed that his Jets did not re-sign fullback John Riggins in 1975....**GEOFFREY GOLDEN** continues to live in a world of magic, princesses and overpriced churros. His new book *Dream It! Screw It! – 30 Years of Rejected Disney Park Ideas from Dipp Disney* (excerpted in *Bystander* #2) just went to #1 on the Amazon Humor charts and is getting raves from actual Disney Imagineers. You can find it at your local indie bookstore, Amazon, or direct from the publisher at devastator-press.com... Though *Bystander* readers know him as co-author of the John Wilcock comics, illustration is just one of **SCOTT MARSHALL**'s many talents; he recently completed a full-length collage score for world-renowned choreogra-

continued next page 🖝

pher Lar Lubovitch ("The Black Rose"), as well as preliminary audio editing for Lubovitch's recent project for the Mikhailovsky Ballet in St. Petersburg, Russia. Can he get you tickets? Probably *nyet*...Scott's Wilcock-mate **ETHAN PERSOFF** is the proud papa of a brand-new book, advertised on page eight: *The Realist Cartoons*, which collects the best comics from Paul Krassner's 1960s magazine. This essential tome will be available from Fantagraphics near the end of 2016. Ethan's website, http://www.ep.tc, is home to his own Comics with Problems and the Realist Archive Project, a complete digital archive of the seminal publication. You can lose days browsing, be warned... **MICHAEL SLOAN**'s "Zen of Nimbus" cartoons were exhibited last month at City Wide Open Studios in New Haven, Connecticut. Catching that, plus a white pie from Pepe's sounds to me like the perfect evening...Los Angeles-based **KATIE SCHWARTZ** has been writing her way through an existential early-life crisis while dreaming of moving to Squamish, BC. (Why Squamish, Katie?) "Career and personal lessons have been mounting at an alarming rate," she says... **STEVE YOUNG** says he's "currently impersonating a college instructor, filling young peoples' heads with TV history, and writing this and that while I wait for the new administration to appoint me Ambassador to Freedonia." ....Bearded, affable **RIVER CLEGG** recently finished the third episode of his crayon-drawn web series, *Betanauts*, which is about astronauts who are bad at their jobs. Go check it out on YouTube. River also tweets a lot: @RiverClegg... Speaking of Twitter, **PAUL LANDER** is way too proud of having accumulated 33K+ followers, and inappropriately boastful of the occasional death threat. The one and only Judd Apatow has retweeted Paul four times, causing Paul's mom to say, "that Judd seems like a lovely boy." ... *Crack! Crack!* That's the sound of the whip: **DAVID CHELSEA** really needs to get back to putting the final touches on *Perspective In Action,* his forthcoming art instruction book from Watson-

Guptill, but first he has to finish peeling and slicing quince so he can freeze them for pie. (Quince is a real thing, David? I always thought it *had* to be a euphemism.)... Hacked emails from the Ecuadorian Embassy in London assures us that "The Government of Ecuador expresses its willingness to cooperate with the security forces in the UK and renews its commitment to protect **D. WATSON**"... Ladies and gents, I'm pleased to announce the first *Bystander* Baby! Illustrator **ERIC BRANSCUM** has just welcomed his second child, Campbell Claire, into the world. This means we have to stay in business long enough to give her the world's greatest summer internship. Welcome aboard little C.C., we'll leave your I.D. badge at the front desk...In addition to scrivening his weekly crop for Mankoff & Co., **KEN KRIMSTEIN** is working on several top secret projects such as [*REDACTED*], [*REDACTED*], and he's especially excited about [*REDACTED*]. If you're intrigued (and how could you not be?) you can see more at kenkrimstein.com... In Spring 2017, Drawn & Quarterly will publish *The Customer is Always Wrong*, the over 430-page sequel to *Over Easy*, **MIMI POND**'s PEN Award-winning and best-selling graphic novel. Mimi is taking it easy right now, judging corgi parades in Chattanooga, Tennessee. She has a new website, mimipond.com; amble over to see the latest... Illustrator **XETH FEINBERG** recently had a series of his relatively large 3D-Plywood-Art-Construction-Wall-Hanging-Paintings shown in a charming little art gallery in the tiny, obscure, upstate

river town of Callicoon, New York. Featuring as they do images of local deer and trees and sullen men and pickup trucks, a number of Xeth's friends and acquaintances claim to have enjoyed this new work immensely and would have surely paid the prohibitive asking prices if any of them had any spare money, which, being his friends and acquaintances, they do not...Living in the O.G. Cambridge, **MICHAEL THORNTON** is shocked! shocked to find an election going on in Ye Olde Colonies. He has been occupied with more important matters, such as writing jingles for his new radio show on CamFM 97.2. He is assured the signal will reach all the way to Grantchester, a brisk afternoon walk away. He recently traveled to the chalk cliffs of Sussex, which he describes as, "A real nice place to end it all."...Finally, **NICK DOWNES** writes, "Michael, I can't imagine your readers being interested in my quotidian existence. After all, when I'm not lying on the couch puzzling out the space/time continuum, I'm down in my laboratory, tinkering with my thermal-infused, photon-blasting, anti-matter disintegration gun. *Bor-ing!* But, thanks anyway."   B

In case there was any doubt whether Merrill Markoe acutally saw the Fabs in concert, here's the program, complete with notes from a teenaged Merrill.

LADIES AND GENTLEMEN, **Lenny Bruce!**

In 1961, Lenny Bruce began a gig at New York's *VILLAGE VANGUARD.* His first time headlining the club:

Hello Hello!

CLAP

CLAP

I DON'T UNDERSTAND how Max Gordon can pay me a grand a week to work here.

He must be a CROOK!

two jazz musicians were just there to visit Powell's
ndmother, who had lived on that street for decades.

DITING NORMAN MAILE

E EARLY DAYS OF THE VOICE, we'd meet every
day at 4am to drive to the printer in New Jersey,
SHEPHERD's voice on radio keeping us awake...

This was always a joyous occasion, until the week of
... *NORMAN MAILER'S FIRST COLUMN* ...

Heh.

Ha!

Heh Heh!

You fat heads!

Hi Jerry,
what is it?

ALI IS STILL CHAMP

The DeadPool count for iconic sui generis celebrities during the first half of 2016 was already too high. Commencing with Bowie, the year got off to a shocking start. I had seen him perform twice. The first time in October 1972 at Santa Monica Civic Auditorium when I was fourteen years old. Next up, or should I say down, was Prince, who was the same age as me. This sort of thing can't help but to insinuate your own mortality, even years after one has cleaned up ones act. The wagon may someday hit a rut and a bump. Out of all of this years dead heavyweights, the only one whom I ever actually met was Muhammad Ali, and this was because of my Dad. I was a little boy in the 1960's living in Los Angeles, while the majority of our extended family lived in the Rocky Mountains. To visit them we would pile into the canary yellow Cadillac 'El Dorado, my old man rakishly behind the wheel with a lit Pall Mall gingerly smouldering as he drove us across the Mojave Desert to glamourous swinging Las Vegas.

As a little boy of seven, I was a hopeless runt of a bookworm, a stumblebum weirdo, who was totally lacking all athletic prowess. Severely near-sighted day dreamer that I was, I was most certainly a stunning disappointment.

My father, a Pacific Theater World War Two veteran, was the Hellenic combination of Dean Martin and Rodney Dangerfield, with a dash of Sandy Koufax for ancient Olympic baseball prowess.

Greeks invented cards. Of course we were going to spend a couple of nights in Las Vegas. It was genetically impossible for my father, or for any of the men in the family, one of whom was an internationally famous mathematician, to drive straight through Nevada without stopping to challenge the fates. Far less than halfway to our eventual destination, it annoyed my mother to no end that we were to lay over in this neon oasis. She was placated with shopping and dinner shows. This was still the Las Vegas of the Rat Pack, so there was no place for kids. I spent the days in the pool, and the nights sitting on the edges of casinos that children were forbidden to enter, jadedly watching the fanciful antics of adults. On this trip we stayed at an amazing space-age palace, the La Concha Motel. It was designed by the famous African-American architect, Paul Revere Williams. Little did we know that an even more famous African-American was just like us, currently a guest. We were about to find out something too cool.

After a few days of cards in Vegas, it was clearly time to hit the road. After all, three-fourths of the journey still lay ahead of us. We got out of bed before the rooster, ate breakfast, and loaded the car. Then my dad and I went into the lobby of the La Concha to check out of the rooms. It was still quite early at this point, so there weren't very many people around. I remember noticing a group of well dressed black men standing together. They were wearing suits that had the essence of a quasi-military uniform with hats that were a cross between a pill box hat and a fez. When suddenly there he was! I recognized him from the television as my dad exclaimed "It's Muhammad Ali! Heavyweight Champion of the World! Let's go meet him!" And so I was swept up in a wave of my dad's bold gregariousness, suddenly finding myself at the feet of one of the greatest athletes ever! Looking up into his smiling eyes, he was instantly friendly and fun. There was joking, teasing, camraderie, and affectionate encouragement to me.

I was merely a child. He was Champ. I was thrilled. We talked about him on the drive and my dad impressed upon me that the one sport I may have natural ability for was swimming. It is true. I'm amphibious.

So I started swimming for a couple of hours every day after school at the neighborhood pool. On the weekends I went to the beach to swim in the ocean.

By the time I was ten, I was on the team and winning races in swim meets. Ribbons and medals displayed on a wall in my room. At swim meets I competed in two races, the individual medley and butterfly. By the time I graduated from high school in 1976, the ribbons and medals hanging in my room looked like a Cheyenne war bonnet. While I looked like someone out of the original Alice Cooper group, a sore point to many on the water sports circuit, it was my own visual trash talk that rattled opponents focus.

Greek men love talking trash. It is part of the culture. If you doubt me, then go read the Funeral Games in the Iliad. Because of this, my dad and I loved watching Muhammad Ali. He was the greatest! at this too. After high school, I could have gone on swimming competitively, but I went to art school instead. A big mistake. My dad died twenty-four years ago. Now Ali has joined him. I live in the Sonoran desert, not far from where Ali lived. Every once in a while I wondered if we may have a chance encounter like the first time, so I could thank him.

TED JOUFLAS *is an illustrator and cartoonist whose work has disappeared internationally. He is the author of many short stories and two graphic novels,* **Scary!** *and* **Filthy.**

Gallimaufry

(n.) a confused jumble or medley.

··········· ◆ ···········

MY CAREER IN A NUTSHELL.

Or, Things Famous People Have Actually Said To Me.

"Do these rolls have caraway seeds?"—Jayne Meadows

"Fuck you."—Elizabeth Taylor

"You just wanted to get in the room with me." — George Harrison

"Get an iron."—P.J. O'Rourke

"Hey you. Writer."—Lloyd Bridges

"Who was better, Roger or me?" — Gene Siskel

"Hey you. Mr. Hollywood." —Rod Steiger

"I was actually stuck in a torpedo tube in the Navy." —Also Rod Steiger

"Don't quit your day job."—Johnny Carson, right before he fired me from my day job.

—Al Jean

SHARE YOUR EXPERIENCE.

Dear Sirs and Madams at Amazon.com: I am writing in response to the email that I received from you on Saturday, March 9th, 2016, at 2:37 PM EST — approximately four minutes ago. As I'm sure you recall, the email began: "Hi Michael J. Weithorn! Will you please take a minute to share your experience?" The "experience" being (as if you didn't know!) my "recent purchase of 2 boxes of HP Copy/Laser/Inkjet 3-Hole Paper, 20lb, Letter Size (8.5x11), White, 500 Sheets (New)."

Before actually responding to your request, I must first confess something (hopefully to one of the more forgiving members of the Amazon family): I nearly deleted your email without even reading it. Rest assured I am not proud of this. But frankly, I sometimes get a bit overwhelmed by the over 200,000 emails I receive each and every day. In most cases what the sender is offering is of no interest to me. That is not meant as any reflection upon them — I'm sure that they are all well-intentioned, honest businessmen, trying to offer others an opportunity to improve their lives. But I've had all the elective surgery I'm going to have, thank you, and returning several hundred emails a day reiterating this has

proven very time-consuming.

At any rate — as my finger hovered perilously over the "delete" button, and began its fatal downward journey... something in your email caught my eye. Who can ever know what, exactly — perhaps it was the friendly, enthusiastic use of my name? "Hi Michael J. Weithorn!"

[Actually, I just went back and checked. Turns out you did not, in fact, use an exclamation mark. Funny how my memory supplied one of its own... funny how we do those kinds of things...]

Perhaps what caught my eye was the tiny but colorful image of the product — two stacked boxes of the aforementioned laser printer paper. Jauntily stacked I might add — the uppermost a bit askew, as if to say, "I may be laser paper, but that doesn't mean I follow all the rules!" (Kudos to the clearly fertile creative minds in your art department.)

But while those two elements may have contributed in their own small ways, I have no doubt that the true light that beckoned me, both optically as well as in the most deeply human parts of my soul, was one word. One word. "Share."

At first, this word was rejected by the most primitive, selfish part of me. The part of me that believes the experience of buying this paper was mine and mine alone. That I possess it wholly, and thus

it is up to me whether I deem to share it with Amazon.com or anyone else. At moments such as this, my narcissism is dizzying.

But thankfully, I soon began to see things more objectively. Was this really just my experience? After all, you received my order. You acknowledged it, processed it, sent the paper on its way. Was this transaction not a very real experience for you, too? A small experience, perhaps — one of hundreds of millions just like it you have every five minutes. But doesn't every experience, even the briefest one, change us in some way? *Vous ne pouvez pas creer de l'experience, vous devez la subir.*[1]

And so, good people of Amazon.com, in one great moment of epiphany I came to understand the deeper meaning of your email. It was... an invitation. An extended hand. A call for you and I, separate participants in the purchase of two boxes of ordinary printer paper, to share our experiences with one another, and in so doing honor the importance of human empathy and communication.

With that noble purpose in mind, on to the business at hand: How would I describe my experience buying two boxes of laser printer paper on your company's website?

[1] *"You cannot create experience. You must undergo it."* — Albert Camus

"I wouldn't call you crazy. But only because nobody uses that word anymore."

In a word, glorious! Sublime. Perfect in all but the minor details. (The paper did arrive some nine weeks after I placed the order using "two-day delivery," and though the product description on your website clearly said "New", the paper had obviously been used before, apparently in the printing of some sort of neo-Nazi propaganda — a virulent, often incoherent diatribe that it was my great displeasure to read this morning. Nobody has to like everybody, but this just went too far.)

But — I digress. Having shared my experience, it is time to turn the tables: Amazon.com, will you please take a minute to share your experience?

I eagerly await your response.

—*Michael Weithorn*

AFFIRMATION #1.

Y'know what? I *do* have nice tits. For a girl.

—*Megan Koester*

HE SAID IT!

"Man is not the sum of what he has but the totality of what he does not yet have, of what he might have. I'm going to buy a dirt bike, is what I'm getting at here." Jean-Paul Sartre, *Situations*, 1939

—*John Howell Harris*

CONCENTRATION SPAM.

Johnny Cash never shot a man in Reno. He did, however, push some guy out of a wobbly Tilt-A-Whirl and covered up the whole thing just for practice. Johnny Appleseed nearly covered North America with rhododendrons before he was caught by vigilantes and later executed in the very same steam chair they still use every day in Kansas. The last passenger pigeon died in 1914. What they don't tell you is Teddy Roosevelt enjoyed the wild rice, too.

I began having impure doubts about print media, broadcasting, and the shrieking voices in my head at around the same time Richard Nixon had President Kennedy imprisoned on the moon. We were a confused country before Wolf Blitzer came along to sort things out for those of us who enjoy the blank promise of a dial tone. Before then, newspapers and radio competed with the same laudable degree of vigor as we see today from cable news and the internet's infinitude of content concerning llamas, Benghazi, and llamas.

There is much talk now about false equivalence in the news and opinion business. And talk about bathrooms. Who should be permitted to go one or two if there might be a three or four?

Should every public restroom require actual resting or contain a Glock-On-A-Chain? And by the way, will that Zika virus gut Caribbean tax havens before they can set up shop in Greenland?

Somewhere on the spectrum there must a channel for older folks feeling nostalgic for white noise. Somewhere a data-miner, pale from a hard day of click, leans back in his Herman Miller chair and says aloud to a headset dial tone "At the end of the day it's all good."

—*P. S. Mueller*

BRAILLE BOOKS ON TAPE.

Voice of reader: "Two vertical dots on the lower left, one in the upper right, then you've got three upper dots, missing the one on the top right. Okay, then there's two diagonal dots, upper left and middle right, then five of the six dots, missing only the one on the lower right..." (*CONTINUES FOR 718 HOURS*)

—*Steve Young*

AFFIRMATION #2.

Sure, that MILF may be hotter than me. But it's a *dry* heat.

—*Megan Koester*

A NEW REPORT...

...from the Department of Health and Human Services says one in twenty American children go to bed hungry twice a week. Conflicting data from the conservative Family Research Council, however, shows that these kids are sent to bed without dinner because they believe in dinosaurs.

—*P.S. Mueller*

FUN WITH FIBS.

Santa Claus, the Easter Bunny, storks, Tooth Fairies, witches – face it, the foundation of a parent-child relationship is lies. Here are a few new ones I'll be trying on my son (who happily for me, has always tested below average on intelligence exams) in the coming years:
• One of every 11 knives is haunted and will turn on you.
• Bananas only rot if the house contains a child who's possessed by the devil.
• No eye contact with the bearded, ever.

• Michael Jordan, Steve Jobs, Albert Einstein, and Michael Phelps all attribute their success to one thing — they mastered the art of staring directly at the sun for ten seconds at a time.

• When you clip your toenails, put them under your pillow. The Nail Fairy will leave money for you, unless the smell of your nails makes him detect penis cancer.

• Wait a second — you DON'T see the wolf standing right there? We better get you to a specialist.

• If the carpet ever stops growing, a plague is coming.

• There is treasure buried somewhere on the grounds of your school — a lot of it, and because schools are on federal land, it's finders keepers.

• The same song my grandma taught me: "If ever you drop a tablespoon, you will be an orphan soon." For Heaven's sake, butterfingers, don't make me die!

• Freckles are ghost-nests — if you find any on your body, scrub, bleach, cut, scald, sand, or burn them off, and for God's sake don't tell anyone.

• The perfect gift for your stepfather — a coffee mug made with boogers you and I have saved over the year.

• Because your great-great-grandfather was part black, it's okay for you to use the N word in front of African-Americans.

—*Dave Hanson*

GLASS HALF FULL.

I don't have a drinking problem. I have a Life's harsh truths solution.

—*Megan Koester*

THERE OUGHTA BE A LAW.

Inside every imported stuffed animal is a tiny mummified kid.

—*P.S. Mueller*

DEAR EMILY: THIS IS A LIST OF THE GRIEVANCES…

…I have with your Palm Desert-adjacent Airbnb, in which I took hallucinogenic mushrooms in last Thursday:

1. In your listing, you made a big fucking deal out of the existence of the house's record player, and its accompanying collection of classic vinyl. But when I went to use said record player, I quickly discovered there was no needle in the cartridge, rendering me unable to listen to your artlessly curated collection of non-essential albums like a tattered copy of "Blondie's Greatest Hits," the Kinks' "Low Budget" (seriously? Low Fucking Budget?) and "Hola," a record released by your white friend's indie pop outfit, the Bandcamp page of which states "draws from influences as varied as Grizzly Bear, The Strokes, and The Kinks." While my inability to listen to these albums is no great loss, especially if the Kinks album your friend's band was influenced by happens to be "Low Budget," I nevertheless am disappointed by your inability to execute the simple task that is keeping your record player in working order, especially in light of what a goddamned hullabaloo you made over it.

2. You yourself are a musician, as evidenced by the placement of a fridge magnet advertising the existence of your latest (and only) release, an EP (naturally) entitled "Indian Summer," the cover of which features a charcoal drawing of a wolf wearing a Native American headdress. To which I ask: Is it still considered cultural appropriation if a wolf is depicted wearing a headdress? Or is the fact that your name is Emily yet you released an EP called "Indian Summer" bad enough?

3. You own the most uncomfortable mattress I have ever had the displeasure of sleeping on, and I used to sleep on a sofa bed. After putting in a good 8-12 hours of arguing, my ex-husband and I would pull the bed out of the sofa and lay, silently ruing each other's existence while staring into the void, for years. The sofa bed mattress sagged in the middle, and the parts where it didn't sag dug into your back—but the thing about this mattress, your mattress, is that there are no sag points, just an endless series of springs and sharp angles generating intense pain, a pain I wouldn't wish on my worst enemy, a pain I wouldn't wish even wish on my ex-husband, and he cheated on me with an Orange County native. I wouldn't wish that mattress on even him, that's how bad it is; and I don't just say that because I want him to be able to sleep because I want him to be haunted by the intangible, impossible horrors of nightmares, the mere ennui waking life elicits not harrowing enough for my taste.

4. One-ply toilet paper? This isn't North Korea—it may be the high desert, but it's still America. Staying in your home was an experience you declared, in rule number one of your listing, I should "have fun" at; watching my piss transform inabsorbent cotton squares into pussy-sticking confetti, however, does not a party make.

5. Your knives. Are dull. So much so, I couldn't competently cut up the hallucinogenic mushrooms in order to ensure

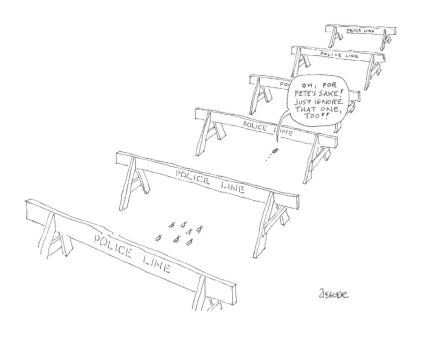

everyone in my party had an egalitarian trip. Cut to (pun not intended) me struggling, hacking away on a carving board, one of the three you provided. (Oh, that's where you shine? In offering multiple carving board choices?) My fellow companions got demonstrably higher than myself and I blame you, Emily, because it's easier than blaming myself.

In sum, I'd give you no stars if I could, but I didn't book the Airbnb, my friend Lil' Mama did, so I cannot rate you. And anyway, I'm part of the problem — I brought my own quinoa and I came to your home solely for the purpose of taking psychedelic mushrooms and I took them and they were pleasant, but apparently didn't work well enough because I'm still upset even though I appreciated the fact that you provided a tube of name brand toothpaste, Aquafresh specifically, which you really didn't need to buy because everything else you provided was of sub-Dollar Tree quality.

I also appreciated the fact that your senseless selection of DVDs contained Swingers, a film I hadn't seen since I was 13 and didn't appreciate at such a young age but appreciate now, on account of how goddamned smart and shrewd it is.

That scene where Jon Favreau's character is sitting on the carpet of his studio apartment, lamenting that he's been in L.A. for six months and feels as though he has nothing to show for it other than the fact that he hosts a shitty open mic but his friend Ron, played by Ron Livingston — who should really be cast in more shit, he's great — tells him he moved to LA because he could see how well John was doing from a distance and if John still feels like a loser, what the fuck does that make him? Holy Christ, Emily. That's a successful psilocybin trip in and of itself.

—*Megan Koester*

AN AVERAGE WOODPECKER...

...could kill a grown man in minutes, if it had a mind to.

—*P.S. Mueller*

AT MONK CHIN RESTAURANT...

...we are deeply committed to a non-oppressive, low-impact, sustainable, carbon-neutral, leaf-to-root green enterprise that feeds the soul as well as the body. Everything we make is derived from non-wheat, non-gluten, low-sodium, worm composted, organically grown whole foods. None of our fruits and vegetables are ever "picked" — they select themselves by freely falling, in their own time, in their own way, from the trees and vines that nourished them. Our flour is milled on a naturally shaped granite stone, not from a manufactured concave millstone. This both reduces carpal tunnel and celebrates erosion.

You'll notice a distinct burnt-wood smell. All of the wood in our floors, tables and the chair you sit in are from recent California brush fires. We have scrubbed the reclaimed wood with distilled water and a non-toxic soap, but you may find black char remains on your arms and skin. This is normal.

The building Monk Chin is housed in was reassembled from a variety of materials gathered from war-torn regions around the world including Somalia, Chechnya and the decomposed tents of the Quileute Native American tribe. The striking and unusual assemblies on the walls are ecologically themed science projects found in the trash of a middle school in a wealthy Manhattan neighborhood.

Please be aware that everyone entering our establishment is greeted with a random act of kindness. This may include, but not be limited to: a hug, kiss, a brief Reiki massage and a blessing in English, Hebrew, Arabic, Hindi or Wolof. However, during this process, our staff will never smile or express any feeling beyond calm and bliss. We do this to culitivate the equanimity necessary for proper digestion.

Each waitperson has been hand-picked to represent the entire cross-section of humanity. Our staff shares in the profits at an equal percentage; however we are *in no way* a traditional business.

Though we do make a profit, in a spiritual sense these credits are actually debits from our souls. On a whiteboard in the back, we are tracking each dollar made as one hour less we deserve to live on this planet. As in Nature, there are no leaders or 'bosses' here; business is conducted through an economic system based upon Japanese Kaizen, the I Ching and the African board game Mancala.

Everyone on our staff receives complete and comprehensive health care from His Holiness Sri Sri Dr. Hashish Shivanandadada, late of the recently

"His last word was the F-one."

closed Willfull Spirit Holistic Health. This includes dental, vision and monthly high colonics personally tuned to each person's biome using Ayurvedic medicine.

Rather than use traditional menus, we present your selections signed by a representative from the hearing-impaired community, eliminating excess noise. For beverages we offer only unfiltered rainwater. Thanks to the recent storms, and a cunningly engineered catch drain on our roof, you'll notice a spigot at your table which you can open at will. *Voila!* Water from the clouds!

(Naturally, if it is not raining, you cannot drink.)

We do not believe it is our duty to judge the herbivores or the carnivores in the food chain, so we do serve meat. However, prior to slaughter our livestock is given a warm bath and a mild chamomile sedative. Our butcher, an artisanal self-mutilator, lacerates his left arm once for every animal he dispatches.

Please note: Our desserts are not made with any sugar, honey, barley malt, or high-fructose corn syrup. We believe dessert should not be a rewarding end to a fine meal, but a reminder of the world's pervasive unfairness and crushing want. Our desserts are carefully blended to create no taste sensation at all; the palate is not only cleansed, it is effectively bleached of all

sensation.

If you must have something sweet, we do offer pieces of raw sugar cane chained to the wall by the communal open toilet. We ask that you suck on them while reading the per capita incomes of the poorest countries in the world, also posted nearby.

If for any reason you are dissatisfied by the spiritual experience at Monk Chin we will not only offer a full refund, but solemnly pledge the business in your honor for 24 hours during the gibbous phase of the next lunar cycle. We will spend this time in sober contemplation, mortifying the body, mind and spirit as is appropriate.

Enjoy your meal. Remember to tip your waitperson. Karma is a boomarang. Peace be with you. *Namaste.*
—*Lee Sachs*

A PROJECT PROPOSAL TO MAKE FRIENDS IN A NEW CITY.

Prepared for: My crippling Social Anxiety
Prepared by: The smallest shred of reason I have left before I draw faces on volleyballs and call it a day
Abstract: In Los Angeles, California, where we have unexpectedly found Broti Gupta, it has proven to be difficult to

perform tasks like "making conversation with a new person" and "not dry heaving directly after, or during, the attempted conversation."

Broti has a history of being very terrified at all times.

In this document, we propose that Broti get out of her pajama pants, buy a hairbrush and attempt to make small talk with a stranger that might amount to a conversation and, ultimately, a cordial friendship that does not involve Broti misconstruing a soft handshake and smile as romantic interest. This proposal includes objectives, a plan of action, a budget estimate and a conclusion.
Objectives: As somebody who has worked closely with you, Broti's social anxiety, I am aware that this project might "literally kill her." To avoid this outcome, I have created a few goals for us to achieve:

1. We will ensure that Broti does not start any more conversations about how long it would take for Disneyland to burn down in a famous California wildfire.

2. We will determine how Broti can attempt to maintain eye contact with another human without saying something weird, like, "Wow, you blink a lot." or "Wow, you never blink."
Plan of Action: In this section, I will detail my plan to go about achieving the aforementioned objectives. I will put Broti in practice scenarios, in situations like a hair salon, or a really long line at

grocery store where she has dropped her "Friends" baseball cap, catching the attention of the person behind her who happens to also love "Friends" and would love nothing more than to talk about how horrible Ross is.

To achieve my first goal, I will train Broti to hear the sentence, "Do you mind if we put heat on your hair?" and not respond with, "Let me just step into one of California's many famous wildfires for some heat." By systematically practicing responses like, "Sure," or, "No thanks, I'm good," I will condition Broti to stop thinking about wildfires.

To achieve my second goal, I will place photos of different people in front of Broti and force her to make direct eye contact with each photo for a good five seconds without grimacing or commenting on the facial expression itself. I will also introduce Broti to the concept of "shared interests," like the show "Friends" and practice conversations with her that do not involve correcting people on Ross's exact professional timeline or shedding angry tears while proving "they were not on a break."

Budget: Well, they say "time is money" and I am not a miracle worker.

Conclusion: Being Broti's reason, I am quite vigilant about the fact that none of this might work. In fact, it could all go to hell pretty quickly. But I can promise you that by this time next year, should this project be funded, we can all be much more confident in the success (or not-so-miserable failures) in future projects like, "Job Interviews" or "Renegotiating the Lease."

—*Broti Gupta*

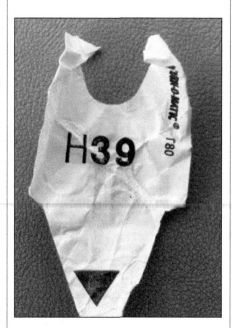

EPIC PRANK!

I took a number at the deli and then just left! I wish I could see the face of the person with number 40 as 39 is being called out until the end of time!

—*Dirk Voetberg*

"Now let's try one without the tusks."

FILLMORE'S ALL-NATURAL EXTERMINATION.

Dear Mr. and Mrs. Grey,
Thank you for selecting Fillmore's! We are Wichita's only exterminators dedicated to providing pest relief the way nature intended. As per your request, the following is a bill for services rendered.

Fly Infestation: $59.99
Spiders eat flies in the wild, so they should be the ones who do it in the home, too. As predicted, the spiders quietly cleared the flies from the target area with zero-carbon emissions and no chemical residue.

Spider Infestation: $135.50
While the spiders diminished the fly infestation, your home had no natural predators to control the spider population, so it became filled with filmy webs heavy with desiccated fly carcasses. Per the contract, our job is not complete until we reach a sustainable solution. As such, we acted on our own initiative and released several dozen leopard geckos throughout your home.

Leopard Gecko Infestation: $625.00
The leopard geckos were able to ameliorate the spider infestation, somewhat. But as this was our first all-natural extermination, we did not anticipate that the lizards would reproduce at such a rapid rate. In response, we deployed 50 rBGH-free cats to counterbalance the increasing numbers of Leopard Geckos.

Cat Infestation: $3,340
While the felines (American Shorthairs from no-kill shelters) diminished the lizard population and had no rBGH, they scurried into unreachable places under the bed and behind the fireplace during the removal phase. None of our all-natural snacks on site (*i.e.* more geckos) were able to lure them out, so we were forced to upgrade our services (*i.e.* release a family of grass-fed cougars).

Cougar Infestation: $12,600
The cougars were not hungry for the cats, because we had already fed them so much grass, but their gnawing, scat and generalized roughhousing did destroy most of the inner workings of your house (appliances, fixtures, portraits, bedclothes, china, etc.). At this point we were unable to safely reenter the premises, so we introduced several well-armed hunters.

Hunter Infestation: $76,200

Using all-natural cougar poison (*i.e.* bullets), the hunters quickly cleared the cougar infestation. Unfortunately, emboldened by their victory, they then dubbed themselves a "militia" and refused to vacate the premises. So we followed up by strenuously lobbying for stricter municipal gun regulations. (Importantly, all our leaflets were printed on recycled paper using soy-based inks.)

2nd Amendment Infestation: $420,500

Following a wildly popular gun safety awareness campaign, the emboldened Mayor imposed fish and game regulations that devastated the local hunting economy. So we ran a smear campaign against him, complete with a Wikileaks-style email dump, to oust him from office.

Faith in Government Infestation: Gratis

Through the smear campaign, we exposed a series of deep-rooted legislative corruptions, undermining the entire municipality's political system. After these highly publicized instances of wrongdoing decimated the public's faith in local Wichita politics, we sought to discredit the media through constant accusations of liberal bias.

News Credibility Infestation: $2,420,800

Having lost trust in the objectiveness of the media, the local populace disengaged entirely, and became woefully uninformed. As a result, we were forced to hire attractive busty news anchors and package segments depicting drugs, violence and sexual misconduct in order to reestablish news viewership.

Gang Infestation: 14 Human Lives

Inspired by the glorified criminal acts portrayed on the news, several street gangs rose to power. The movement took to initiating children, including those of some of our employees (*i.e.* Craig). In response, we were forced to mastermind another even more radical gang based out of your house and instigate a feud among them. Unfortunately, the feud ran too deep. As the number of shootings increased around your neighborhood, we hired a clown to come by to ease the tensions. Admittedly, we were grasping at straws here, but, it was all-natural.

Clown Infestation: $80

We extend our deepest sympathies to friends and family of Sneaky the Clown.

BANX

"I'M GETTING BLACKBERRIES AND WHITE CHOCOLATE WITH A SUBTLE HINT OF TOASTY OAK."

Locally sourced flowers were purchased and sent to the family through Greener-FlowerDelivery.org.

Fly, Spider, Leopard Gecko, Cat, Dog, Cougar, Hunter, 2nd Amendment, Faith in Government, News Credibility, Gang, and Clown Infestations: $39.99 plus tax

The prostitution, drug-trafficking, and shootings continued to spread, and the leopard gecko population once again spiked as the cats escaped through the bullet-shattered windows. To combat the growing radical movements, lack of trust in media, constitutionality disagreements, bears (oh yeah, we added bears at one point, I forget when exactly), cougars, housepets, lizards, and bugs that hadn't all been eradicated throughout holistic methodology, we ultimately decided to gas your house with a standard-issue chemical insecticide. So, no more flies!

TOTAL DUE: $2,934,380.48 plus tax

Please remit payment at your earliest convenience.

—*Zack Bornstein*

MY BROTHER'S WEDDING IN THREE MONOLOGUES.

On the Phone to My Sister Belle:

So he's finally marrying the girlfriend? …Fiancé, *whatever*. That word is so revolting, it's vile, it's like "make love." Either you fuck, you screw, or you have sex. "Make love" sounds creepy, needy and molestery. (*mocking*) "Will you make love to me?" Belle! Remember the schmuck who said that to me after dating him for a week?! I told him to drop dead…

Of course, I'm being overdramatic. Have you ever met me? I'm your sister Katie, nice to meet you.

You can tell Emmett I'm not getting on a plane for this. I'll have to go shopping in August when it's hotter than a hooker's pussy on a Saturday night, and spend money I don't have to attend a wedding I don't want to go to. I HATE MALLS. I HATE PEOPLE. I HATE EVERYTHING.

…I don't care.

Okay, I care. I'm happy for him. But why do people insist that others attend their weddings?! They're the epitome of radical, institutionalized selfishness. They're horrifying. They're worse than menstruating during a colonoscopy.

…I know, I'm a romantic.

Belle, Again. One Day Later:

I have to give a fucking toast? What am I going to say?!

Good idea, I *will* think of it like a tweet. A 4,000-character tweet.

Why are they having it at a country club? We're Jews, we don't golf, and we have taste buds. WAIT! DON'T HANG UP YET. Answer me this, Belle: when have you ever eaten good food at a country club? P.S., chicken cutlets are not "food."

This whole thing is an act of aggression.

Where am I? I'm at the salon getting my hair done...Because you told me to get my fucking hair done. Wait, the groom is calling me.

He's calling to say I shouldn't use the word "vagina" in my toast? Why would I ever — because no cursing? Vagina is not a curse! Plus, cursing is our family's second language. This is censorship! WHAT IS HAPPENING TO ALL OF US?!

I'm picking it up. Hold on.

Emmett, why would I use the word vagina in your toast?...You've seen it on my Facebook wall?! And no fucking swearing? Why?

...Grandmothers have heard it, Emmett. Grandmothers have HBO.

...I don't walk around inserting my vagina into conversation. I just happen to be comfortable saying *vagina*. That does *not* make me "a loose cannon"!

No. I'm sorry. I won't promise anything. You ask me, you take your chances. I'm sorry everybody else has stage fright.

Six Months Later:
Emmett and Amelia, congratulations on your nuptials! I hope that you will be as blissfully happy together as me and my vagina are. May you have as many adventures together as we have. Like for example, the three blokes from the New Zealand Rugby Team. Anybody wants to hear more, come over to my table.

Amelia, you feel a bit asexual to me, then again, I think my brother has a Madonna/Whore complex. So maybe that's perfect, I don't know. Anyway, I got you a pocket rocket. It's the gift that's moving slightly.

Emmett, though we've only discussed my vagina at your request, I got you two books, *Clitology* and *She Comes First*, so you and Amelia's vagina can cultivate a deeper, more meaningful relationship.

Grandmothers, could you wave? Still alive? See, Emmett — you had nothing to worry about. Enjoy your chicken cutlets, everybody.

—*Katie Schwartz*

FUN MUSIC FACT.
Pharrell's smash hit "Happy" was written in a fit of utter rage.

—*Dirk Voetberg*

DAILY THOUGHTS FOR THE UNENLIGHTENED.
Don't let things be just as they are. Why would you do that when they're so shitty?

Ask yourself: Who am I going to fix today?

Stop not judging. Not judging is for people who don't know one thing from another.

Don't listen to your inner voice. Listen to that outer voice, the one that says,

"How many times do I have to ask you for the check?" and tells drivers who can't hear you, "Get out of the passing lane, you motherfucker!"

The present moment is a nice place to visit, but there's no reason to live there.

Think of a painful event from the past, or a fear of something terrible happening in the future. See how easy it is! Now think of another.

Count your blessings. Then count your friends' blessings and see how many more they have.

Have you stopped focusing on your breath?

Be there then.

If the universe wanted you to be at peace, don't you think it would have arranged it already?

—*R.D. Rosen*

WHATEVER HAPPENED TO MANNERS?
Yesterday a server at the restaurant where we ate lunch dropped his tray, shattering plates and glasses everywhere. And I swear I was the only one who clapped and hooted and yelled, "Nice job!"

—*Dirk Voetberg*

A NEW WORLD RECORD AT THE 2016 "AIN'T NO SUNSHINE" WORLD CHAMPIONSHIPS.
Official: "Contestant set. Take your breath. Ready."
(PISTOL SHOT)
Contestant: "Ain't no sunshine when she's gone, and this house just ain't no home, anytime she goes away. I know,

"Oh, Lord no, I'm not a professional terrorism expert."

I know, I know, I know, I know, I know,
I know, I know, I know, I know, I know,
I know, I know, I know, I know, I know,
I know, I know, I know, I know, I know,
hey, I ought leave young thing alone,
but ain't no sunshine when she's gone."
(ENORMOUS INHALE)
(WILD APPLAUSE FROM CROWD).
—*Steve Young*

SLOPPY THE SLAVE.

He's the dirtiest and laziest slave in
the entire Roman Empire. And he's a
liar and sneak as well. But just look at
those big, sweet, brown eyes of his...
You can almost hear the other slaves
saying things like:

Head Slave
Sloppy, look at this vomitorium.
It's filthier than before when everyone had just finished vomiting
in it! What have you been doing
all morning? Vomiting?

Sloppy
Didn't I clean that?...Wait, I
thought I cleaned that...I must
have cleaned something else by
mistake...I thought I cleaned that
though.

Head Slave
You're hopeless. Oh, don't bother.
I'll do it. Hand me that ragmop...

Sloppy
Awww. The ragmop. I'd pick it up
and hand it to you but my back is
really killing me...it's been going
in and out...

And you can almost hear the Roman
Empire falling all around when the head
of the Pretorian Guard yells at Sloppy:

Head Guard
If you think for one minute you're
going to be allowed to attend the
Slave's Spring Picnic/Jamboree,
you've got another think coming...
And don't give me that sad-eyed
look. It won't work this time...Now,
stop it, Sloppy. I mean it. Don't you
give me that look. Stop looking at
me like that. Quit it!...Ooowww-
ww...okay, you can go to the slaves
Picnic/Jamboree. But at least wear
something clean. Something not
covered in slave vomit!

—*Brian McConnachie*

"Mother says we need to talk."

WHERE THE MONEY WENT:

1) 17,000 pairs of silk underwear
2) A 2 MPG Cadillac Monstra
3) Off-planet betting
4) The Segway racing circuit
5) A holographic 50s-style world for mom
6) Tuition for grad studies at The School of Rock
7) Donated for polar bear habitat you don't dare visit
8) Total strangers on the phone
9) Several hundred Saudi princes
10) Hiring Jack Nicholson to record my phone message

—*P.S. Mueller*

THE SEVEN MOST COMMON COGNITIVE DISTORTIONS.

Everyone's guilty once in a while of
indulging in unhealthy ways of thinking, like dwelling on negative feelings,
blowing things out or proportion, or assuming that coworkers are very interested in hearing about a recent dream. But
when left unchecked, these patterns of
distorted thinking, known as "cognitive
distortions," can lead to anxiety, depres-
sion and insufferable Facebook posts.
The key is to identify these thought patterns early, and work on ways to untwist
your thinking. To that end, here are ten
common cognitive distortions:

OVERGENERALIZING: One of the
most common cognitive distortions is
overgeneralizing, when we come to a
general conclusion about something
based on a single incident. For example:
"I got a bad grade on a test, therefore I
am not a smart person." Or "My online
date wasn't as good a fisherman as he
indicated in his profile. I can trust no
one." These are toxic thoughts that can
make your life miserable.

BIRD MIND READING: Another
common distortion is bird mind reading,
which is assuming you know what birds
are thinking about you. For example, if
a bird switches branches when you walk
by, you might assume that it believes
you are dull or uninteresting. A duck
which swims away quickly on a pond
might lead you to conclude that it is
angry with you. "I threw bread into the
pond, but that duck didn't eat it. Is that
duck angry at me? Did I say something
bad? What's that duck's problem?" Bird
mind reading is usually emotionally
loaded.

SOUP LABELING: This is when we
generalize one or two qualities of a soup
into a judgment about the soup as a
whole. For example, if an order of soup
is tepid or greasy, we might say "This
soup is a loser. This soup will never
succeed." A can of soup with too little
flavor might be labeled a jerk, or an
asshole. "I hate that soup. I hope I never
see that soup again." Soup labeling is
not only irrational and reductive, but is
also unfair and untrue. Remember that

soups are complex and fallible, and no soup should be reduced to a label other than what is specified on the can.

RUPAUL REASONING: You assume RuPaul's feelings and emotions necessarily reflect the way things really are, regardless of observed evidence. "RuPaul is afraid of lizards, therefore lizards are dangerous and can hurt me." "RuPaul believes my partner is unfaithful, therefore I must break up with them." RuPaul Reasoning is most common among RuPaul.

NEGATIVE SCOTTISH BROGUE-ING: With this type of cognitive distortion, all of your thoughts are filtered through a negative Scottish Brogue. "Ye cannae do this, laddie, ye are nae smart nor hansomish enow!" Or "Ye are but a wee bairn in yon officing, best ye should lay ye down in native peat and expire, loike." When these judgments overwhelm, try to substitute a positive thought. "Hae a hantle blythesome! Ye are yin oot bonnie great able."

PILOTIC TRANSFERENCE: Pilotic transference is a distortion when you tell yourself that you could do a better job of flying the plane than the current pilot. But when you actually storm the cockpit and try, your confidence disappears, and you crash the plane into a barn containing your whole family.

When such thoughts arise, pause and think: "This plane has autopilot. What are the realistic odds of my killing my family in a barn fire?" The answer may be reassuring.

DINOSAUR FILTERING: This is when we take the negative aspects of dinosaurs, such as their big teeth and scariness, and filter out all positive attributes like their awesome claws and the fact that many of them can fly. An example of dinosaur filtering:

Martin is at a fancy business dinner with the other executives of his Fortune 500 Company. They are discussing the company's quarterly earnings and each employee's contribution to its overall growth. Suddenly, Martin's boss announces: "Did you know that some dinosaurs are faster than cheetah cats? I kid you not." Martin immediately tenses up. Cheetah cats are so fast and scary, probably the fastest cats ever, and they can catch deer no sweat. That means dinosaurs are even scarier than that."

Martin's fear of dinosaurs ruins his business dinner. But if he corrected his thinking, he would realize that they are so big and cool, and so many of them you can outrun. To counteract Dinosaur Filtering, draw pictures of your personal favorite dinosaur, or gather friends and ask each to discuss their favorite thing about dinosaurs.

CATASTROPHIZING: "Catastrophizing" is when a person convinces herself that something that has happened, or will happen, will be so awful and unbearable that she won't be able to handle it. Unfortunately, this instinct is correct 100 percent of the time.

BILLY BALDWIN BLAMING: Self-explanatory.

SHOULD STATEMENTS: This is when you criticize yourself or others for not conforming to what you believe a person should or ought to do. "I should exercise. I must win this race. I shouldn't have cast judgment on that can of soup. I shouldn't have assaulted that duck at the pond. I must apologize to my boss for screaming hysterically about dinosaurs during dinner. I shouldn't have blamed the downfall of my marriage on Billy Baldwin, even though RuPaul says it was his fault."

Cognitive distortions are powerful, but they do not have to overpower you. Whenever you face a frightening or negative thought, ask yourself this: What's the worst that can happen? In most cases, the answer is the same: All of your family members will perish in a barn fire. But recognizing these distortions puts you one step closer to having a happy, healthy internal life, and convincing your therapist to write you a prescription for a coveted drug.

—*Jocelyn Richard*

OUR ADMISSION FEES:

Adults: $15
Children: $15
Seniors: $15
Senior with Small Child: $15 (each)
Uniformed Military Personnel: $15
Military Personnel in Civilian Clothing (with military ID): $15
Wheelchair Patron: $10 (plus $5 for use of wheelchair ramp)
Disadvantaged Student with Scholarship to Vocational School: $15
Blind: $15
Blind in One Eye: $12 (plus three-dollar Eyepatch Tax)
Deaf and Dumb: Please inquire at box office
Group Fee (10 persons): $150

—*Jack Handey* **B**

BY DESERT ROSECEA

PICK-UP ARTISTRY VOLUME IV

Listen up, you guys — he has a SYSTEM

Hey my bad boys, bang bros, and anti-cucks! Desert Rosacea here! The man, the myth, the pick up artist legend! It's time for another pick up art column. I'm bringing you all the tips you need to bang your mark and forget about missing mom's love. You don't need her! You don't need anybody! Here are some tried and true methods to getting with lady holes:

DRESSING LIKE A GOTH PIMP

You know what women love? Furry top hats. Really really long top hats. Their bodies react inadvertently to anything that reminds them of a penis. You need to remind her that you have a penis as much as possible, because women forget. Get a cane. Get a sword. Get a cane sword. Get a sword that looks like a penis. Wear one long, pointy earring. Wear so much eyeliner they think you were peeping through a dirty glory hole.

ACTING LIKE HER FATHER

You know who women want to sleep with? Their fathers. Dress like her father. Bellow like her father. Glue on a few random gray body hairs. Do that weird throat clear burp thing her father does. Tell bad puns about football or lawn mowing. Only talk about lawn mowing. Explain your lawn mowing techniques in great detail. Get a lawn and make her mow that lawn. Say Hillary Clinton 'just makes you uncomfortable.' Invite her over to watch City Slickers. Wear the same cologne as her dad (you don't have to ask, it's always Drakkar Noir).

FOLLOWING HER AROUND WITH A BUNSEN BURNER

You know women are afraid of fire? Show her your power! Remind her of the dudes who used to talk over her in science class. This is known as gaslighting and it's super awesome, I

totally researched it on urbandictionary, bros.

GETTING A GIRLFRIEND

You know who women go after? A guy who's disinterested and taken. Ask out a girl. Take her someplace nice. Buy her a personalized gift. Find out what she likes in bed and do it generously. Share in her hobbies. Stay up many nights just talking and sharing your feelings. Move in together. Get a corgi. Ask her to marry you. Have a beautiful rooftop ceremony with a rustic fall color scheme. Grow old and die together. Have a joint funeral. Ladies will be lining up to make out with your romantically satisfied corpse. Your dead wife (RIP Janice, light of your life) will have no idea what hit her!

DOING IMPROV

You know what there aren't enough of? Men who've taken a level 1 UCB class and keep talking about it. Women love that. Bonus: You can jump into a scene to squeeze Madam President's boobs. That'll totally help you with your discomfort about Hillary Clinton!

SLAPPING A BOOB ON THE FREAKIN' TABLE

You know how to show your dominance? Slap a boob on the table! Go to a crowded bar. Order a manly drink, like a straight whiskey on fire. When the bartender doesn't respond quickly enough, slap a big silicone boob implant on the table and say "THAT'S WHY!" It doesn't have to make sense. That's not what women are responding to.

There we go my female-trainers! My lioness tamers! My man meats! All the best tips to getting ladies in your bed where they belong and can never, ever leave you like mom did. Come back, mommy! I made you macaroni art! **B**

HANA MICHELS
*(@HanaMichels) was raised by Jewish therapists and has been seeking validation through comedy ever since. She's been published in **Paste**, **Funny Or Die**, **Reductress** and others.*

BY BRIAN McCONNACHIE

WHO AM I?

C'mon, guess

I am friend to the working man and the part-time working man and the working woman on maternity leave with her feet up and the college girl on spring break at that place in Mexico they show on TV and makes her parents crazy with worry. I make the uniforms that people who have to wear uniforms wear. I write the songs that people bravely sing when they're looking through their closets wondering what uniform they're supposed to put on that day.

I steer the rigs. I drive the trains. I tug the boats. I fly the planes. I lower the gates at railroad crossings (but not when I'm driving the trains). So please, if you hear a train coming and you think I'm driving it and the gate is still up, for God's sake, stop! Use your heads, people. I can't be in two places at once. At least not under these figurative circumstances...well, actually, I can. But if I did it for your crossing, I'd have to do it for all the crossings and I just have too much on my plate right now. To say nothing about all the crap I have stored in my wheel house. Packed to the rafters. So let's just say I'd rather not and leave it at that.

Continuing on, I am both tomorrow and yesterday and I'm that Saturday that feels like a Sunday, because Friday was a holiday. I am a hot dog and a soda pop on a summer day; I am a mighty crown roast of veal with a pitcher of margaritas later that same evening. I am a car alarm, a smoke detector, a cell phone and a beeper all going off at once telling everyone in no uncertain terms: Switch to plan B! Hurry. I am the last cigarette lighter that still works on the Mir space station.

Do you still not know who I am? Really?

Okay, we can keep going. I have time. How's this? I'm an enigma wrapped in an artichoke stuffed in a riddle dreaming of a powerful conundrum. Anything yet?

I am the determination that will finally compose the overdue official Song of Soccer that will be as jolly as "Take Me Out to the Ballgame" and will extoll the many wonderful bones of the foot while pooh-poohing the hand and all its fancy la-de-da digits in chorus after chorus after chorus. I am the midday calm following that summer day of hot dogs, crown roasts and margaritas when someone flings open the door and yells: Are you going to get up, or what?

I am the porter who takes your bags. I am the chambermaid who wonders: What the hell went on in here last night? I am sometimes with you and I am as often missing when you turn around wondering: was there someone standing behind me just now?

I am at the dry cleaners when you think I'm at the ATM and I'm at the DMZ having a BLT when you think I'm at the IRS. OMG! WHOA. Now, all of a sudden I'm turning into a mystery stapled to a riddle that's taped to a gypsy's thigh who stalks through the good farmer's artichoke patch wondering and wandering, wandering and wondering.

Do you know now? Still nothing? I'm running out of clues here.

What if I just said I was a dog sticking its head waaaaay out of the car window loving the breeze? You'd like that. I'd like that too but it's a little too dead on. Or is it?

Let's try this...

I am the frustration of a little child who can't get the top off the aspirin bottle and I am the happiness of another little child who has been inhaling nitrous oxide for the last four minutes. I am the ever-changing size of Greenland on world maps and every time you see me, you go quietly puzzled, thinking: Jeeze, look at Greenland! I don't remember it being that big. What do you suppose happened? I am the typos in your resume you were positive weren't there. I am the flammable string-in-a-can for people who are drunk at a wedding and think its amusing to shoot it at the bride and groom (though this a part of me I am least proud and rarely mention.)

Now, anybody? You've got that blank stare. I'll give you one last chance: I am the two legged person hearing how the one legged person's missing leg can still itch. Day after day the missing leg is itching and missing; missing and itching.

Still nothing? Okay. That's it. No more hints for you.

I am the, "Handling," part of, "Ship ping and Handling," that you've always wondered about and has been robbing you blind for the last forty-eighteen years or so.

Surprised?

You shouldn't be.

BRIAN McCONNACHIE is Founder and Head Writer of *The American Bystander*.

BY STEVE YOUNG

STAR WARS SCRIPT MEETING

Someone just like Yoda, only not, and maybe sexy

September 15, 2016 meeting, *Disney headquarters* In attendance: *Writers and producers R, S, K, J*

R noted that *Star Wars Episode VIII* is well into production, yet several crucial plot points have yet to be figured out. Elements need to be superficially new, yet comfortingly familiar. Summary of discussion follows.

DEATH STAR/STARKILLER PROGRESSION

S and K reviewed the progression thus far: The Death Star was a moon, then *The Force Awakens* raised the bar with a Starkiller Base planet. The group agreed that an even bigger, more impressive "space ball of death" is necessary, but how to up the ante?

K pitched that the next movie's "death ball" should be a star. All admired the logic of this, yet there was concern that a star would be "too bright to look at," "too hot to work in," and "would burn up all the computers and stuff."

R suggested a "large planet with a ring which acts like a circular saw and cuts other planets in half with a prolonged high-pitched grinding noise." Deemed "appealing," yet rejected because of the annoying sound as well as the fact that "everyone would have to wear safety goggles."

S offered the notion of "a giant ball of planets" which could be held together by "gravity beams or girders or something." J jumped on this, pointing out that "the giant ball of planets could shoot fire, or planets, or planets on fire, or planets on fire that themselves shoot lasers." All agreed this was "awesome" and "different without actually being a new idea." APPROVED

SPACE BALL OF DEATH'S DESTRUCTION/NICK OF TIME

K observed that the Death Stars and Starkiller Base are invariably destroyed by the rebels with mere seconds to spare. How many seconds prior to disaster should the rebels destroy the Giant Ball of Planets?

R said "three seconds, just like always." Agreement that the three second option would go over well with fans, yet worry that Episode VIII could miss an opportunity by not trying something slightly new.

K proposed "four seconds." Dismissed as "not high enough stakes due to the extra remaining second."

S suggested "one second." Shot down as "too unbelievable."

J pitched "two seconds." Extensive back and forth about this option.

After nearly an hour, S suggested "two and a half seconds." "You could have a digital timer showing tenths of a second," pointed out K. "Fractional seconds would be a great way to keep the franchise fresh," agreed R. General enthusiasm and relief. APPROVED

REBEL ATTACK STRATEGY ON THE GIANT BALL OF PLANETS

All parties quickly agreed that the rebels' attack strategy did not require an update. "No need to reinvent the wheel on everything," noted R. "Cinematically, there's nothing more satisfying than a small overlooked vulnerability involving ductwork." APPROVED

ADORABLE ROBOT

J reviewed the variations thus far: R2D2 is a cylinder with a rounded top, BB-8 is a ball with a rounded top. What would be an appealing form for the next adorable robot?

continued ☛

STEVE YOUNG *(@pantssteve) is a veteran Letterman writer who's also written for The Simpsons. He recently worked on NBC's Maya & Marty variety show, and is teaching a course at NYU's Tisch School.*

S suggested a cube with a rounded top. Admiration for the boldness of this idea, yet worry that "we've established that adorable robots have to have a bottom section that's sort of round."

K's attempt to bring triangles into the discussion resulted in acrimony.

Brief excitement over R's pitch that the bottom part of the adorable robot could be "pear-shaped," followed by discouragement. "We've never established that this galaxy has pears," noted S.

Following a long silence, K pitched "a ball of balls with another ball on top." The group quickly seized upon the obvious merit of this idea. "It could be named like ZP-72 or ZP-73 or whatever," suggested R. After intense debate, the name "ZP-75" was chosen as the name of the adorable robot shaped like a ball of balls with another ball on top. APPROVED

ADORABLE ROBOT SOUNDS

Once again, the group agreed that a new approach was not required. Unanimous acclaim for "the usual 1970's computer bleeps and bloops, with perhaps a slightly more melancholy whistle." APPROVED

OMINOUS BLACK VILLAIN MASK/HELMET

S observed that the ominous black Darth Vader mask and helmet had been followed by the ominous black-with-silver-highlights Kylo Ren mask and helmet. Clearly a new-ish, slightly-less-iconic variation is needed for the villain being introduced in Episode VIII, Bulp Mofo.

K suggested "a plain black helmet, but the mask has lots of blobs and protrusions near the eyes, in case we want to have a story line about Bulp Mofo's limited peripheral vision." Lukewarm response.

R pitched "a really mean-looking welding mask, because maybe Bulp Mofo does a lot of welding." J reminded R that as currently conceived, the Bulp Mofo character once enjoyed welding but has lost interest.

PIG LATIN

COGITO ERGO SUM

MEMENTO MORI

PERSONA NON GRATA

ARGUMENTUM AD HOMINEM

CARPE DIEM

E PLURIBUS UNUM

AD ASTRA PER ASPERA

DEUS EX MACHINA

GRANT SNIDER

J proposed that Bulp Mofo wear "a large, round black helmet with a stem-like appendage on top, triangular holes for the eyes and nose, and an oblong mouth cut-out with jagged edges."

Proposal met with awkward silence.

S ventured: "How about even though Bulp Mofo no longer is interested in welding, he still wears the welding mask, because he's evil and refuses to give it to a welder who's just starting out and could really use it." APPROVED

TO BE ADDRESSED AT NEXT MEETING

Bulp Mofo's light saber needs to have a superficial difference. Two parallel beams for no particular reason? Beam color: plaid? ▣

BY QUENTIN HARDY

EVERYTHING HAS A PROBLEM

Forget exploration — it's time for an intervention

EUGENIA LOLI

In the time it takes to read this sentence aloud, the universe has expanded by approximately 314 miles per megaparsec, or roughly 8.9 million miles. Slightly more, if you had to clear your throat, or drawled. Meaning that once again, the universe is at a greater size than at any time in its nearly 14 billion-year history.

Except for now.

And now.

It can't stop.

We must, as a species, face facts: We live inside a narcissist, and a dangerous one at that. Infinitely hot, infinitely dense, always expanding. Always commanding the fundamental laws. It would be sad, if it weren't so alarming. The universe is like some out-of-control celebrity we all know is headed for trouble, unless somebody *does something*.

But what? We're complicit, too — codependent, even. The more attention we pay the universe, the more it seems to crave. We obsess about where it came from, where it's going. New celestial telescopes, NASA's paparazzi, strain to discern its secrets, compelling the universe to keep us guessing.

For example: We find one Earth-like planet in a distant galaxy. Huge deal for us, lots of attention for the universe. So of course, a couple of months later, to get rid of the loneliness and emptiness inside, the universe reveals another, and people go crazy again. Then there's another, and another, until liquid water-bearing planets whirling around G-type main sequence stars are as common as candy corn. What was thrilling becomes…embarrassing. Needy. Almost pathetic.

Did you know that during the Big Bang several other promising dimensions got crushed to insignificance? God forbid someone else would come in for some attention! And talk about boundary issues — our sharp-elbowed universe is growing without end, totally insensitive to anyone else's need for space. Plus, it never seems able to account for its supply of dark matter. Where did you get it? What's it made of? Who gave it to you? Don't ask the universe; it's as mute as a sullen teenager.

We know what this is: It's cry for help. Seeking something it can never find. The universe is 56 billion light years across. It has 100 billion galaxies, 300 sextillion stars, and uncounted millions of half-completed dust clouds. Universe, you're not even finishing them!

It's like what they say in AA: one is too many, 300 sextillion is not enough.

Once the Universe had youth, looks, and the romantic-sounding promise of heat death. The equivalence of all mass and energy, that's moody, intriguing — a good way to meet girls. After a while, though, women get tired of pie-in-the-sky dreams, and start looking for something like a plan.

At a density of one hydrogen atom per four cubic meters of volume, the universe is beyond stretched; you can see it's had work done. But what do you expect? If you rule your existence with physical constants that favor gravity among the four fundamental interactions, you pay a price. It's not our fault gravity is a drag.

Look, I'm not judging here: The universe came from nothing. No strong male role model, no loving maternal figure. There's obviously going to be some instability at the beginning. But at a certain point, you have to take responsibility. Are you growing, or are you distancing yourself from intimacy? Fourteen billion years ago was then, this is now.

The universe has to want to change. It has to do the work, go to meetings, maybe even rehab. It's not going to happen overnight — you want an eternal manifestation of all Number, Form, and Motion to pull its act together, you should have caught it in the first few picoseconds. But change is real: Just stay positive, focus on the healing. One planetary rotation at a time.

QUENTIN HARDY *(@qhardy) is a Deputy Technology Editor at* **The New York Times.** *For a number of years, he was the in-house Maoist for a show on Fox News.*

BY MIKE REISS

WHAT AM I DOING HERE?

Bourbon Street: where America goes to ogle

I've been married for twenty-eight years, and the key to my happy union is that I surrendered free will around the time the Berlin Wall fell. It's kind of ironic: The East Germans gained their freedom at the same time I lost mine. But it seems to be working out well all around.

Case in point: The February after Hurricane Katrina devastated New Orleans, my wife said, "I think we should go down there for Mardi Gras."

I said what I always say when my wife has a horrible idea. I said, "Good idea," and off we went.

We stayed in New Orleans with our friend Merrill, a Cajun so old and so tiny, even his racism is cute. For example, we were watching *Conan* with him and Merrill said, "Believe it or not, I like this show." Then a black guest came on. "And now I don't," he added.

Adorable.

The night before Mardi Gras, we met Merrill's nephew Kenny. Kenny had just been released from Louisiana State Prison for "a crime he didn't commit." And these had clearly been hard years for him: His front tooth had been knocked out. He flinched a lot for no reason. And at some point, someone clearly had set Kenny on fire.

Every fiber of my being told me to stay the fuck away from Kenny.

My wife said, "We should bring Kenny to Mardi Gras with us!" And I said, "Good idea." And so we did.

We arrived on Bourbon Street at eight in the morning, Fat Tuesday. The streets were already crowded with fat drunken men. I had hoped to see lots of topless women, but that's illegal in New Orleans.

Instead, there were hundreds of shirtless women, their breasts painted with amusing designs: cartoon bombs, Confederate flags, eight-balls — a panoply of motifs. By Louisiana state law, this counts as clothing.

My wife — my conservative wife, my Harvard-educated wife — said to me, "I wanna get my boobs painted!" And I said… well, you know what I said.

I handed fifty bucks to a Hell's Angel I'd never seen before, and he disappeared into an alley with my disrobing wife. Ten minutes later she emerged with a *Playboy* logo painted on each breast.

Immediately — immediately! — ten thousand men with cameras materialized and began snapping photos of my wife. I tried to be the supportive husband, posing with my wife.

But it became clear no one wanted me in the pictures. In fact, men handed me their cameras, so I could shoot them hugging my topless wife.

I had become William H. Macy in *Boogie Nights*. For those of you who don't remember the film, he played a meek husband cuckolded by his pornstar wife. The film ends with Macy killing his wife and then himself.

My wife was going through changes of her own. At first she was brazenly going, "Take a good look, boys!" But soon she was saying, "Just take the picture, okay?" And finally, "Why won't you monsters leave me alone?"

I'm describing this change in real time. My wife went from blushing ingénue to burnt-out sex kitten in forty-five seconds.

At this point I needed to use a bathroom. There were now eight hundred thousand men on Bourbon Street… and three toilets. The shortest line was three blocks long, so I did something I'm not proud of. I went to the head of the line and told my wife, "Give them a show." She shook her breasts angrily — breasts can shake angrily. The crowd cheered and I strolled into the restroom.

So now I was Eric Roberts in *Star 80*. If you don't remember that movie either, Eric plays a man who pimps out his wife to *Playboy* for personal gain. That film also ends with the hero killing his wife and then himself.

By this point, my wife and I were mad at each other, mad at ourselves, and mad at mankind. And it was only 9:30 in the morning.

And then we saw Kenny. Poor jailbird Kenny. He was having the time of his life, drinking Hurricanes, catching Mardi Gras beads, and snapping pictures. And I thought if we could make a poor soul like Kenny so happy, maybe we weren't such bad people.

I said, "Kenny, you having a good time?"

"Yes sir," he replied. "I'm gonna come back next year and bring all my wives."

"All your wives?" I asked.

"Yeah, there's my first wife — she and I still get along fine. And then there's my current wife."

He added, "But my second wife — she was a bad person. That's why I killed her."

And my wife whispered to me, "Let's get the fuck away from Kenny."

I said, "Good idea." And for once I meant it. B

MIKE REISS *has won four Emmys and a Peabody during his twenty-six years writing for* **The Simpsons**. *Reiss also co-created* **The Critic**, *and created Showtime's hit cartoon* **Queer Duck** *(about a gay duck).*

BY P.S. MUELLER

IT'S GETTING HARD TO FIND A GOOD HENCHMAN THESE DAYS

Not all that long ago you could have a car, a house, wife, kids — the whole ball of wax — and still afford to keep two or three henchmen on hand for a little extra weekend muscle. Whenever the Clustersons next door got all hopped up about the Arabs or whatever and started tuning up their fleet of lawn mowers at three in the morning, I could send Wally and Joe over there to give free knuckle rides. Heck, they were happy with whatever they made on the mowers. The trade in hot Toros was a going thing at the time and a good henchman could work his way up. Inside of a year or so, Wally was living in the Clusterson place with a couple of his own gorillas.

In those days having a henchman around was like having an extra member of the family, ready at a moment's notice to slap around any ringmaster passing through town who let his clowns talk dirty to your kids. It was good to have a guy who could make it absolutely clear to the counterfeit lobster people that it was not OK being counterfeit lobster people. And it didn't matter that Uncle Jasper had a Circuit City name tag that didn't say "Jasper" tattooed on the back of his left hand or that he was thrown out of Ireland, twice. He was my henchman and I let him use our garage to sell supplies to other henchmen, because when you have a good henchman, it's all good.

Except when it's not all good. I mean, henchmen do age out of the business, and replacing one can be tricky. This will probably sound cold to you, but I have found the best way get rid of an over-the-hill enforcer is to audition a long-lost unacknowledged son with an ax, or taser, to grind. Otherwise, you have to go through the complicated process of arranging passports, travel, hotel reservations, and just leave the guy in a Dublin bus station. And it's really not good at all when your henchman gets just enough past it that you find him neatly folded in with your shirts one day, delivered with no charge by the drycleaner you sent him to rough up a bit.

More than anything, I blame change and technology for the sad and gradual fade of the loyal henchman. Nowadays people rent Uzbek sociopaths by the hour. There's an online startup where you can simply download an app and they send you a young kid all tricked out like a Bond villain. Big deal that he's got some kind of fancy gun and can somersault in and out of more trouble than anybody had in mind. Fierce loyalty, however, will cost extra and may lead to a series constantly escalating car chases when all you wanted to do was lean on a fry cook who gave you the fish-eye.

Not only is it getting hard to find a good henchman these days, it's getting harder to make a call on using one. I mean, newsboys used to be a dime a dozen, but now a guy like me really needs to think long and hard before having one beaten half to death. What if we run out of newsboys? And do I want to be known as the character who drove the last newsboy into the daycare racket? Background checks? Do I really want to know if the henchman I hire today was once a doctor in Swaziland? Am I worthy of the responsibility of deciding whether my henchman should breathe heavily into the face of that spindly little man who used the wrong polish on my wingtips? A good henchman can't help me with any of this.

P.S. MUELLER *has been publishing cartoons since 1969. He co-created The Onion Radio News and still serves as Anchor Doyle Redland to this day.*

BY MERRILL MARKOE

HOW TO GET ALONG WITH FRIENDS AND RELATIVES STUPID ENOUGH TO BE VOTING FOR THE WRONG SIDE

David Chelsea

DAVID CHELSEA

Aren't we all getting a little sick of living in a country that operates like a big dysfunctional family, so perennially disgusted by large numbers of our fellow Americans that we have no choice but to dread any mandatory gatherings? Isn't everyone fed up with living in our Two-Conspiracy-Theory System, wherein the minority party spends four years trying to prove how the majority party is dismantling the Constitution and hastening the apocalypse?

I bring this up because the holidays will soon be upon us — no matter when you are reading this, holidays are always about to descend. That means lengthy, utterly unavoidable encounters with friends and family members possessing horrible political opinions.

This year, before it all starts again, I suggest we rethink things. What choice do we have? We're all in this together (though I can be talked into excluding those who refuse to stop texting). In the name of finding more civil, adult ways to communicate, allow me to offer a few time-tested methods for defusing any potentially explosive social encounters with theoretical loved ones definitely on the wrong team.

1: HIT THE GYM

Before attending any social event that will require close contact with contentious people, be sure to get lots of physical exercise. Studies have found that "tired" looks almost exactly like "peace and serenity."

2: BE A GOOD SPORT

It's important to call a moratorium on partisan gloating. No more rocking back and forth while whistling and making that face with the raised eyebrows and the faint smile that says, "Don't look at me. I'm just sitting here, minding my own business!" Remember, a well-timed silence can be just as infuriating as name-calling.

3: DIAGNOSE

At the same time, be sure not to take someone else's explosions of political rage personally. A good way to do this is to identify which childhood traumas may be at the root of the terrible choices this person is making. Prepare yourself for unavoidable social events by perusing the American Psychiatric Association's Diagnostic and Statistical Manual of Mental Disorders. The more quickly and specifically you can affix someone with an official personality disorder, the easier it will be to shift building hatred into simply finding this person pathetic.

4: SOOTHE, DON'T SEETHE

When the impulse to punch begins to arise, instead reach out, hug the person gently and whisper, "I hear that you are angry. Know that I'm here for you if you want to cry." As you dry their tears, pull out your phone or iPad and share a few of your favorite animal videos — taking care to avoid those where the animal does something so dunderheaded that it could be construed as a metaphor for Donald Trump. (For example, that Golden Retriever who lets tennis balls just bounce off his head.) Try to stick to cats sleeping someplace unexpected: A paper bag! A sock drawer! A frying pan! Or anything featuring a wallabee! Hey! Where has all that seething hatred disappeared to now?

5: THE PITY PARTY

Here's an idea that always works: Have a pity party! Everyone is always saying, "Don't have a pity party," but that's because most people don't know how to throw a good one! The key is to invite a large number of vain people prone to histrionics about thinning hair, gaining weight or developing nasal labial folds. No matter what their political inclinations, anyone exposed to this crowd for more than a few minutes will be unable to focus on anything but an escape plan.

6: RYAN? OR CHRIS?

If none of the above seems to help, remember that the best counterattack is an unexpected response. When your uncle says, "People don't want a democracy. They want a babysitter!" pause for a minute, then say, "I can't figure out who you remind me of. What's the name of that blonde actor in his 30's who is always the reluctant superhero? Bradley someone? Or is he a Ryan? Or a Chris?" This will launch you into a tranquilizing, endlessly distracting whirlpool full of undifferentiated celebrities and their interchangeable movies, which can last as long as necessary.

7: REDIRECT AND DISTRACT

Remember that living in The United States means more than just feeling like a helpless piece of a paralyzed system drenched in political hatred. Its also about learning to navigate a culture that routinely exalts the worst in products and entertainment! In the end, the key to getting along with people on the wrong side of the aisle is finding the things upon which everyone can agree, thus redirecting all the free-floating anger toward a common enemy. That means it's your responsibility this and every holiday season to be sure to invite any friends or relatives with substance abuse problems to every one of your gatherings. In the event that they forget to attend, as is often the case, have at the ready a list of the names of obnoxious anchor people, conspiracy theorists and reality show contestants as a way to redirect acrimony. There is nothing like a rousing discussion of worthless pop-culture egomaniacs to remind political antagonists how much common ground they still share.

In closing, I would like to propose that before the next Presidential election, we the people of the United States (if we are still calling ourselves that by 2020) create a brand new methodology for dealing with the days on which we vote. Since we now live in an era where our elections, like our winter holidays, are both nerve wracking and endless, why don't we soften things a little by adding a few beloved holiday trappings? How about Election Trees, red, white and blue lights, and a post precinct-closing gift-giving celebration? If all those who picked the winning candidate had to buy gifts for those whose candidate lost, it would soften the blow, stimulate the economy and simultaneously create new, more traditional avenues for releasing partisan anger. After all, there's nothing like a national holiday celebration that involves the giving of gifts for bringing Americans together in a terrifying ritual of pent-up rage. **B**

MERRILL MARKOE *writes for all the existing forms that still allow the long spelling of the word "you." For a lot more information than you may require, why not peruse Merrillmarkoe.com.*

The Ballad of Three-Bean Salad

.... ◆ ....

Words by MIKE REISS *Art by* SARA LAUTMAN

This is the tale of a woman named Midge
  Who invited friends over to play some bridge
She made some brownies, and she made a cake
And then Midge made a big mistake…
She made a three-bean salad.

Three-bean salad
Such a mean, mean salad,
You're better off sticking with a nice green salad
If you've ever seen salad, still you've never seen salad
That's as mean as a three-bean salad.

Now no one's kinder than a kidney bean
And the green bean can be calm and serene,
But when you mix them with a garbanzo
The three of them go completely gonzo…
Loco, that is…
Those beans go nuts.

Midge put those beans on a serving dish
And offered some to her friend Trish.
Trish said, "Ooh, I've got to try it!"
And the beans said, "Trish, go on a diet."
  "You're fat, girl."
"*Muy gordo*."

Then that three-bean salad made a heck of
  a mess
On Bonnie's blouse and Dinah's dress
The girls ran out without playing bridge
And Midge put the beans right back in the fridge

Midge tried again on Christmas Day
She put those beans out on the buffet
The three-bean salad cried, "Bah humbug!"
Then they poured the gravy all over the rug
They dumped all the stuffing right in the eggnog
And fed the turkey to Midge's dog
The dog liked that
Midge did not.
But she didn't give up…

Midge brought the beans to picnic lunch,
Potluck dinner, Sunday Brunch
And folks would eat the other food
But the three-bean salad was just too rude.

So Midge put the beans in a covered plate
Where they've been since 1968
And now they sit in back of
  the freezer
Victorious as Julius Caesar
Still uneaten
Still unbeaten.

Three-bean salad
Such a mean, mean salad,
You're better off sticking with a nice green salad
If you've ever seen salad, still you've never seen
  salad
That's as mean as a three-bean salad.

And that's the Ballad of Three-Bean Salad.   B

IN 1600'S ITALY, THE CHURCH RULED. *MICHELANGELO MERISI DA CARAVAGGIO* LONGED FOR THE FAME AND MONEY ITS COMMISSIONS WOULD BRING. BUT THE POPE'S WAY TO PAINT WAS NOT HIS WAY. HE WAS THE ONE THEY CALLED THE PAINTER OF...

"COMMON BODIES WITHOUT BEAUTY"

THE OFFICIAL ART OF LATE 16ᵗʰ CENTURY ITALY WAS MANNERISM—THE GAUDY PASTRY THAT MASKED THE DARK CULTURE OF THE INQUISITION.

CLOUDS OF RICOTTA

FLYING BABIES WHO GOT MUSIC LESSONS...

THE ROLLING OF EYES

IN FANCY DIAPERS.

BRIGHTER BRIGHTS, WHITER WHITES!

WHEN YOU GOTTA GLOW YOU GOTTA GLOW

MAMMA MIA!

POSES, GESTURES AND GENUFLECTION

BIG CROWD IN MARY'S BEDROOM— THE ALL-TIME GREATEST SAINTS ALL-STAR TEAM

AFTER CARLO SARACENI (1570-1620) DEATH OF THE VIRGIN

THINK THE BURNING OF GIORDANO BRUNO— HIS HERESY WAS TO MAKE THE SACRED ORDINARY.

Christ was not God. He was just a good magician.

APPLAUD!

DURA FLAME

AND THIS TOO, WAS THE HERESY OF MERISI, WHO TURNED OUT THE LIGHTS OF PAINTING AS THEATER, MADE PRETTY BOYS WITH DIRTY FINGERNAILS INTO SAINTS AND PUT PROSTITUTES INTO THE SHOES OF THE VIRGIN.

HE WAS A COUNTRY BOY TRYING TO MAKE IT BIG IN ROME, AN APPRENTICE IN THE BUSY STUDIO OF GIUSEPPE CESARI—

Nice grapes Merisi, but paint out the holes in the leaves.

That's how it is. Look. Bugs ate the leaves.

Paesano, if you want to be good you have to learn from the masters.

Cesari, see those people outside?

"Nature has supplied me with enough masters."

Hey gypsy, you want to make a few scudi?

MERISI'S PAINTING, GYPSY FORTUNE TELLER, WAS RADICALLY REAL AND NEW.

You're painting low life.

"A good man knows how to imitate natural things well."

HE FOUND ADMIRERS AND PATRONS AMONG THE ART SMART CLERGY. CARDINAL DEL MONTE INVITED MERISI TO LIVE IN HIS HOME...

BENVENUTO

Thanks to Cloudy With A Chance of Meatballs, **Ron Barrett** *is a cult figure among eight-year-olds. His* Excessive Alphabet, Avalanches of A's to Zillions of Z's *is due this year.*

COMMISSIONS FOLLOWED. THE FIRST, *THE CALLING OF MATTHEW*, WAS PAINTED DIRECTLY FROM LIFE. UNLIKE OTHER ARTISTS, MERISI DID NOT MAKE A PRELIMINARY DRAWING AND USED ONLY ONE SOURCE OF LIGHT.

THE STARK REALITY OF THE PAINTING BECAME THE TALK OF ROME. LISTEN TO A JEALOUS RIVAL, GIOVANNI BAGLIONE:

Fabulous, everyone! Matthew, give me that "Who, me?" look. Beauti-ful, baby! Jesus, your arm's sagging.

Cecco, raise the lamp.

The painters in Rome were taken by the new-ness of it and... hailed him alone as the only imitator of life.

BUOYED BY HIS SUCCESS, MERISI MAKES HIS FIRST MISSTEP. THE ALTARPIECE, *MATTHEW AND ANGEL* IS REJECTED BY THE PRIESTS. MERISI DESPAIRS —

They said "it had no decorum nor did he look like a saint... his feet rudely exposed to the public."

AND THEN, LITIGATION IS ADDED TO INJURY: THE "TALKING STATUES" OF ROME ARE PLACES WHERE SATIRE AND PROTESTS ARE POSTED. IN AUGUST 1603 THE PAINTER BAGLIONE AND HIS ASSISTANT MAO FOUND THEMSELVES SUBJECTS OF A BIT OF DIRTY DOGGEREL POSTED ON PASQUINO.

"So take your drawings and sketches to Andy the grocer or wipe your ass with them or stuff them up Mao's wife's cunt since you're no longer fucking her."

BAGLIONE CLAIMS MERISI IS THE AUTHOR AND SUES HIM FOR LIBEL. MERISI IS CONVICTED AND JAILED. IN THE NEXT TWO YEARS HE IS ARRESTED FIVE MORE TIMES FOR...

STREET FIGHTING!

INSULTING THE POLICE!

VAFFANCULO!

DESTRUCTION OF PROPERTY!

HERE'S MY RENT!

ASSAULT WITH A DEADLY WEAPON!

ASSAULT WITH A DEADLY VEGETABLE!

COMMISSIONS CONTINUED, AS DID THE REJECTIONS. *THE DEATH OF MARY* WAS REFUSED BY THE CARMELITES. AS BAGLIONE PUT IT:

"She looks like a whore swollen from a suicide in the Tiber."

UNLACED BODICE!

IN FACT, SHE WAS LENA ANTOGNETTI, MISTRESS TO SEVERAL PROMINENT CLERICS AND OFTEN A MODEL FOR THE MARYS OF MERISI.

BUT IT WAS THE MAN, NOT THE ART, THAT WAS ABOUT TO BECOME ANATHEMA TO THE PAPACY.

IT BEGAN ON THE TENNIS COURT, WITH RACQUETS.

Where's the ten scudi you owe me?

Come and get it.

IT ENDED WITH A SWORD THRUST TO THE YOUNG GENTLEMAN'S GENITALS THAT LEFT HIM DYING AS MERISI RAN.

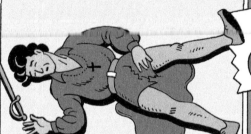

THE POPE PLACES A...

BANDO CAPITALE

ON MERISI. NOW ANYONE IS AUTHORIZED BY THE CHURCH TO KILL HIM.

MERISI RUNS TO NAPLES. HE PAINTS THE MONUMENTAL *SEVEN ACTS OF MERCY,* IN WHICH CARITAS RO-MANA, ROMAN CHARITY, BREASTFEEDS A STARVING PRISONER.

HOPING FOR SOME CHARITY FROM ROME FOR HIMSELF, MERISI SAILS TO THE FORTRESS HOME OF THE ORDER OF THE KNIGHTS OF SAINT JOHN OF JERUSALEM — MALTA.

A KNIGHTHOOD WOULD GIVE MERISI CLOUT IN ROME, MAKE IT EASIER TO GET THE PAPAL PARDON THAT WOULD REMOVE THE *BANDO CAPITALE.* THE GRANDMASTER KNIGHT WAS WILLING TO HELP. HE DUPES THE POPE INTO SIGNING A DECREE THAT PER-MITS THE KNIGHTING OF A CERTAIN MURDERER, WHO, UNKNOWN TO IL PAPA, IS MERISI.

GIVEN A COMMISSION BY THE ORDER, THE NEWLY KNIGHTED MERISI ASSERTS HIS STATUS BY SIGNING IT IN THE BLOOD OF THE SEVERED HEAD OF ST. JOHN AS...

Fra (BROTHER) *Michel Angelo*

f Michel A

BUT BROTHERHOOD IS SHORT-LIVED. MERISI COMMITS AN UNSPEAK-ABLE CRIME. HE IS DECLARED *NEFANDO* — "A FOUL AND ROTTEN MEMBER" AND DROPPED INTO...

THE GUVA!

A DEEP HOLE CARVED OUT OF THE ROCK.

SOMEHOW MERISI ESCAPES THE GUVA, SCALES THE CASTLE WALLS BY NIGHT...

AND SAILS TO SICILY.

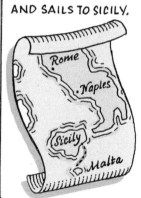

Rome

Naples

Sicily

Malta

ON MALTA A STOOL IS DRESSED AS MERISI, PUT ON TRIAL, FOUND GUILTY AND STRIPPED.

MERISI, UNAWARE OF HIS EXPULSION, LEVERAGES HIS KNIGHTHOOD INTO A COMMISSION— *THE RAISING OF LAZARUS.* HE DIGS UP A MODEL..

GORGONZOLA!

WHEN TWO ASSISTANTS REFUSE TO POSE HOLDING THE ROTTING CORPSE, MERISI USES HIS PERSUASIVE POWERS.

HIS PAINTINGS DETERIORATE INTO SLAPDASH TECHNIQUE AND VACANT COMPOSITIONS. ANGERED BY A SLIGHT CRITIQUE, HE SLASHES LAZARUS.

"I can do better."

WANTED FOR HIS PAINTINGS AND HUNTED FOR HIS LIFE, HE RETURNS TO NAPLES, WHERE HE IS PROMPTLY DISFIGURED BY AN ATTACKER.

LOCANDA Del CERRIGLIO Home of Good Times

MEANWHILE, BACK AT THE POPE—

Cardinal Gonzaga, your request is granted. Michelangelo Merisi is pardoned.

NEWS REACHES MERISI AND HE SAILS FOR ROME.

These paintings will be my "grazie" gift.

BUT THE SHIP MAKES AN UNEXPECTED STOP...

We're nowhere near Rome!

I said "Get off!"

AN AMBUSH AWAITS.

ON THE THRESHOLD OF PARDON AND REDEMPTION, MICHELANGELO MERISI DA CARAVAGGIO IS KILLED.

HIS BODY WAS NEVER FOUND. HIS MURDERERS NEVER KNOWN. KNIGHTS OF MALTA? ENEMIES FROM ROME?

SO MANY SUSPECTS.

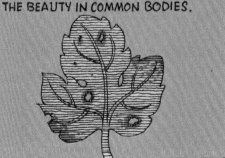

THE SHIP WITH HIS PAINTINGS RETURNS TO NAPLES, BUT MERISI'S NEW REALISM TRAVELS NORTHWARD, WHERE IT BECOMES A REMBRANDT, A GOYA AND ALL THE ARTISTS WHO WERE TO FIND THE BEAUTY IN COMMON BODIES.

B

Dirtbags

The "Dirtbag" series began by imagining Shakespeare as performed by a teenaged dirtbag cast. Things took off from there — here are a few of her finest.

Dirtbag Macbeth

THREE WITCHES appear on the heath.
WITCH #1: have you ever killed a pig
MACBETH: what
WITCH #2: do you want to be king
MACBETH: king of what
WITCH #3: king of jerking off
jesus
"king of what"

————

MACBETH: do you think I would make a good king
LADY MACBETH skateboards across the hall
LADY MACBETH: king of jerking off maybe

————

MACBETH is sleeping. LADY MACBETH pops a BMX wheelie over their bed.
LADY MACBETH: you should kill duncan
MACBETH: idk
LADY MACBETH: or i could do it
MACBETH: what
LADY MACBETH: it's fine i'll do it
brb
LADY MACBETH wheelies offstage.

————

MACBETH: arent you going to wash your hands
LADY MACBETH: lol what
no
MACBETH: you're covered in blood
LADY MACBETH: let's make out
MACBETH: what

LADY MACBETH: it'll be metal as hell
MACBETH: i don't know
LADY MACBETH: god it's like being married to my fucking grandmother

————

MACBETH is sleeping. LADY MACBETH straddles his body and kisses him while smearing blood across his face.
MACBETH: WHAT THE FUCK
LADY MACBETH: i wanted to make out
now we're even
MACBETH: EVEN FOR WHAT

————

LADY MACBETH: you know who else we should kill
MACBETH: who
LADY MACBETH: that one guy
your friend
MACBETH: feel like we've already killed a lot of my friends
LADY MACBETH: then we could throw a PARTY
and make out

————

BANQUO'S GHOST appears.
MACBETH: don't do that
come on
don't look at me
don't fucking do that
don't be an asshole
BANQUO'S GHOST does not move.
MACBETH: fucking asshole

————

SEYTON: your wife is dead
MACBETH: who

SEYTON: your wife
Lady Macbeth
MACBETH: yeah well
she probably would have died tomorrow
SEYTON: what
MACBETH: or whenever
i mean we're all going to die someday
so it doesn't really matter

Dirtbag Athena

ZEUS: sweet hells does my head ache
ATHENA [*bursts out of his skull in full armor*]: surprise, fucko
ZEUS: what the hell
ATHENA: i didn't feel like being born regular so here i am
parent me
ZEUS: what the HELL
ATHENA: you got something on your forehead champ
ZEUS: I —
ATHENA: SOME AFTERBIRTH
get it

————

CLIO: wow Arachne you're like REALLY good at weaving
ARACHNE: ahaha thank you!!
CLIO: no I'm serious
you're amazing
ARACHNE: haha
I guess you could say I weave like Athena herself
ATHENA [*appearing suddenly in the*

continued ☞

————◆————

Mallory Ortberg is "Dear Prudence" for **Slate**. Her second book, **The Merry Spinster**, is being published by Holt in 2017. She says it's going to be "SPOOOOKY, like Shirley Jackson."

fireplace]: the fuck did you just say

ATHENA: let's have a little contest
humans versus gods
whoever weaves the best tapestry wins
and just to make sure everything is fair
i'll be the judge
ARACHNE: that doesn't seem —
ATHENA: i'm literally the god of fairness
i'll definitely be fair
contest starts now

ATHENA: wow that's like, REALLY good
ARACHNE: …thank you
ATHENA: except for what's with that
weird dark spot in the middle?
ARACHNE: what weird dark spot?
ATHENA [*stubs out cigarette in the
middle of Arachne's tapestry*]: that one

ARACHNE: all right
i'm done
what's your verdict
ATHENA: i mean
it's good
i mean, it's fine
i just don't really get why you felt like you
had to turn yourself into a spider for it?
ARACHNE: what?
ATHENA [*turns her into a spider*]: do
you see what i mean
it was a weird choice

"You're it!"

Dirtbag Beowulf

HROTHGAR: ah, Beowulf
welcome to Heorot and the land of my
people
we have heard of your deeds from across
the sea
BEOWULF: yeah it's no big deal I pretty
much swam here
UNFERTH: Is't so?
I heard you were bested by Breca in a
swimming contest not three w —
BEOWULF: yeah actually I once held my
breath for like a million hours
it was crazy
my friends weren't even worried because
I fight guys underwater like all the time
until it had been like two days
and then they were kind of nervous
because I'd never held my breath that
long before
but it was no big deal, I was just holding
my breath
UNFERTH: I —
BEOWULF: yeah so I only lost to Breca
because I was too busy beating up sea
monsters
underwater
instead of swimming
UNFERTH: well
I suppose I —
BEOWULF: so how many Grendels have

you killed so far, Unferth
anyone here who's killed a Grendel raise
your hand
that's what I thought
GRENDEL: more like Gayowulf
BEOWULF: hey Grendel
say hi to your mom for me
BEOWULF: anyone here who's killed a
Grendel raise your hand
[*he raises Grendel's torn-off arm*]
raise the hand of however many Grendels
you've killed
hey Unferth
stop hitting yourself
stop hitting yourself with Grendel's hand
UNFERTH: my lord, I should never have
doubted you
and I'm sorry I — please stop doing that
BEOWULF: i'm not doing anything
i'm not even touching you
Grendel's touching you
BEOWULF [*skateboarding out of the
mead-hall*]: Hwætever
FIFTY YEARS LATER
DRAGON [*dying*]: more like
[*coughs weakly*]
Gayowulf

Dirtbag
Teddy Roosevelt

TAFT
TAFT
what is it, Mr. President
COME INTO MY OFFICE
I WANT TO BENCH PRESS SOMETHING
why don't you bench press your presi-
dential desk
I ALREADY BENCH PRESSED IT
sir, I don't want to be bench pressed
AM I THE PRESIDENT OR AREN'T I
IF I WANT TO BENCH PRESS THE MEN
IN MY CABINET
IT'S FOR THE GOOD OF THE NATION
AND YOU SHOULD BE GRATEFUL FOR
THE OPPORTUNITY TO SERVE YOUR
COUNTRY
NOW GET IN HERE AND ASSUME THE
POSITION
yes, sir
I'LL BENCH PRESS ANY AMERICAN
I WANT
yes, sir

————

TAFT
GET IN HERE THIS INSTANT
THE BOYS IN THE WAR DEPART-

MENT ARE LETTING ME USE THEM
TO RECREATE THE BATTLE OF SAN
JUAN HILL
AND WE NEED YOU TO PLAY SAN JUAN
HILL

TAFT
what is it
DO WE OWN THE PHILIPPINES
do we what
DO WE HAVE IT YET
no, sir
I believe the Filipinos have it
WELL I WANT IT
how do you propose to get it
I PROPOSE TO STRIKE ANY MAN WHO
TRIES TO STOP ME SOUNDLY IN THE
FACE IS HOW
I PROPOSE TO ACQUIRE IT THROUGH
THE STRATEGIC USE OF COLD BATHS,
STRENUOUS MOUNTAIN HIKES, AND
BARE-KNUCKLE BOXING
I PROPOSE TO RIDE YOU LIKE A PONY
ALL THE WAY TO MANILA
please don't ride me like a pony, sir
IF YOU LET ME RIDE YOU LIKE A PONY
I SHALL APPOINT YOU SUPREME
COURT JUSTICE
sir, you promised me that last Christmas
after you used me as a footstool during
the White House reception
I MEAN IT THIS TIME
NOW OPEN YOUR MOUTH SO I CAN
GET THIS BRIDLE FITTED

TAFT
TAFT
WAKE UP YOU WALRUS
what is it
THERE'S A WAR ON AND YOU DIDN'T
TELL ME
where's a war
we're not at war
NOT HERE, YOU BLOATED MUSTACHE-
HOLDER
IN RUSSIA
i
yes
there is a war in Russia
WELL I'M GOING THERE TO PUT A
STOP TO IT
their war is with the Japanese, Mr. Presi-
dent
it's not with us
IF I CAN'T HAVE A WAR
YOU CAN BE DAMNED SURE THE RUS-
SIANS AND THE JAPANESE AREN'T
GOING TO HAVE ONE

"Are you a gambling man?"

wait a minute and I'll send someone from
the State Department with you
TOO LATE, TAFT
I'M ALREADY ON MY WAY
GOING TO DO LUNGES ACROSS THE
ATLANTIC
SHOULD BE IN MOSCOW BY NOON
I'LL WIRE WHEN I GET THERE

TAFT HAVE YOU HEARD OF THIS
STANDARD OIL BUSINESS
yes, sir
THEY'RE A MONOPOLY
yes, sir
THAT ISN'T SPORTING AT ALL
no, sir
BRING ME STANDARD OIL
I'M GOING TO PUNCH IT MANFULLY
IN THE FACE
sir, Standard Oil is a trust, not a person
you can't punch a trust in the face
OH CAN'T I
TAFT, WATCH ME BECOME THE FIRST
MAN TO PUNCH A TRUST IN THE FACE
THEN WRITE IT DOWN
IN YOUR OFFICIAL WHITE HOUSE
NOTES
"TODAY THE PRESIDENT PUNCHED A
TRUST IN THE FACE"
all right
"QUITE SOUNDLY TOO"
I will
"WITH AN EXCELLENT RIGHT UPPER

CROSS"
yes, sir
"CAN'T PUNCH A TRUST IN THE FACE"
FORSOOTH
I'M THE PRESIDENT
I CAN PUNCH ANYTHING

TAFT WHAT'S GOING ON
WHY ARE THESE BOYS TAKING MY
THINGS OUT OF THE OFFICE
you're not the President anymore, sir
WHY ON EARTH NOT
you've already served two terms
we had another election
WELL WHO IS THE PRESIDENT NOW
I am, sir
WHAT
YOU SWOLLEN CARAPACE
YOU'VE NEVER EVEN RIDDEN A BEAR
NOR STRUCK A MOUNTAIN
NOR EATEN A LIVE HORSE WHILE
RIDING ON THE BACK OF A DIFFER-
ENT HORSE
HOW CAN YOU BE PRESIDENT, YOU
HUNK OF UNDERCOOKED LIVER
I am the President now
and I'm afraid you're in my office
and I'll have to ask you to leave
WELL I
I'M GOING TO GO TO AFRICA AND
KILL EVERYTHING I SEE THERE **B**

Chapter One:
Downturn Abbey

"I have not read this book."
H. M. THE QUEEN

Downturn Abbey

an unauthorized parody by Michael Gerber
author of *Barry Trotter and the Shameless Parody*

Now that we're a couple of issues into this thing, people ask me fairly often, "How did *The Bystander* happen?" Sort of with the same tone of voice you might use if you walked into someone's apartment and it was filled with thousands of Monarch butterflies. Not a bad thing, exactly, kind of beautiful in fact; but odd, definitely odd. And indicative that maybe certain levels of forethought and respect for consequence, what guidance counselors used to call *maturity*, are not in play.

I can spot this attitude a mile away — beneath the grin, there's a certain narrowed-eyed bracing-oneself look — and whenever I see it I want to say, "I'm right there with you. I know every possible place to sit is covered with butterflies. Please do not crush them with your ass."

Anyway.

The best and quickest and least psychologically fraught answer to the question of how *Bystander* came to be is *Downturn Abbey*. In 2012, I wrote a book-length parody of the BBC costume drama, at that time kicking arse and taking visiting cards all over America, courtesy of PBS. *Downturn* was a natural project for me; I'd given the *Young Frankenstein* treatment to Harry Potter in 2003, Narnia in 2004, and Dickens in 2007, to various amounts of acclaim and lucre.

But in addition to my apparent compulsion to graffito all aspects of British literary culture, I have an enduring interest in the Edwardian period and World War I, both topics at the heart of *Downton*'s first season. And who isn't interested in death by copulation? I don't mean "interested in" as in "eagerly seeking" — that's between you and your Fetlife profile — but more a morbid fascination. To date, I know almost nothing about Nelson Rockefeller, but I do remember that he came and went at the same time.

What does all this have to do with *The American Bystander*? Everything. *Downturn Abbey* was the first project I ever funded via crowdfunding, and its rapid success made me believe that smart, design-intensive print humor projects could be funded via Kickstarter. Without that successful dry run, the whole *Bystander* thing might have felt too daunting; or I might have spent the rest of my life plodding about the carpeted corridors of Manhattan in a fruitless quest for capital. *Downturn Abbey* showed that not only was *Bystander* possible, it could be fun.

Consider this, then, the first butterfly. —*MG*

CHAPTER ONE.

The Heartbreak of Male Heir Loss.
(April 15, 1912-June 1912)

I well remember my first day at Downturn Abbey. It was the morning after "the big canoe went down." Not what I took much notice of that—no one related to me was on the *Titanic*. In fact, no one related to me was anywhere. Back in those days, parents were a luxury, like protein, and I had neither. That's why I showed up at the back door of Downturn, my one shoe shined, my hair combed, ready to begin a new life.

At eight, I was a bit of slacker, but a natural impulse to better myself and avoid the considerable inconvenience of starvation had impelled me to the classified section of *The Urchin* magazine. Under a quiz called "Fifty Forelock-Tugging Ways to Drive Your Betters WILD," I spied a small advert for a "tray-boy" at the crumbling, half-wild estate just up the road from Ripping Foundling Home.

> "Do you dream of a better life?
> Travel? Excitement? Adventure?
> Good luck to you. In the meantime, we require a tray-boy.
> Long hours, little pay. Must be alarmingly small for age.
> Full set of fingers required; mutes preferred.
> Apply to Mr. Cussin,
> Downturn Abbey."

As my eyes played over the tiny print, my calorie-starved faculties sputtered out a glorious future. First I'd obtain a left shoe. Then I'd rise up through the ranks, eating exotic, nutritious things like carrots, and rubbing shoulders with the great personages of the era… And then, perhaps, one of those personages would see something in me, a spark, something that recalled themselves at my age, and my chance would come. A chance to make good; a chance to show the world what I, Percival P. Percival, was put on this good green Earth to do.

For those of you unfamiliar with the workings of a great house — and in the case of Downturn, I use the term loosely; just how loosely you're about to find out — a tray-boy is a young male of approximately waist-height who follows members of the household, wearing a metal sideboard supported by his shoulders and crown. He is, for want of a better term, a sort of mobile end-table, and as human furniture, occupies the absolute bottom of the pecking order. But all work is honorable — so *The Urchin* serials had told me—and I was determined to be the best tray-boy Downturn had ever had.

"You'll be back before nightfall," predicted the Home's Matron, as fat as all of us were thin. "Say hello to Colin for us, will yeh? If he's still breathin'."

This was not idle speculation. Colin, an older, bigger boy and Matron's favorite, had for some years been employed holding up Downturn's subsiding North Gallery. Fortunately, Tray-boy is not as physically demanding a position as Foundation-lad, and

offers much contact with the family. But this can be a disadvantage, if one cannot show discretion. These articles are, I suppose, a response to that — a clearing of the mental mechanism after eight years spent observing the most incredible things in silence. To be all of thirteen, for example, and see Lady Marry dance *Le Sacre du Printemps* in the altogether — I don't mind telling you, I nearly burst a blood vessel. And stroke was not the only peril; I later found out that the boy I was replacing, a chap roughly equidistant between Colin and myself, had succumbed to ether fumes while helping the Earl of Cantswim anaesthetize some butterflies. But I didn't know that then. Lucky for me, I didn't know anything. When I rounded the path and saw the estate for the first time, I was sure that great things were ahead.

• • •

I was met at the back door by Mr. Cussin, Downturn's fearsome butler. "You must be the new tray-boy. Come in." Something about the bright Spring morning must have offended him, because Mr. Cussin then uttered a string of words so foul that I assumed only orphans knew them. At first, I was frightened by the oaths and imprecations that constantly issued *sotto voce* from the man as he navigated a world that did not come up to his standards. Later, I learned it was a habit over which he had no control, any more than Mrs. Snughes could prevent falling asleep, or Craisy, Downturn's dogsbody, could stop herself from setting fires.

"Not the drapes, Craisy!" Mr. Cussin barked. "The fireplaces!"

"Sorry, Mr. Cussin."

"Never mind that. This is Percy, our new tray-boy."

"Pleased to meet you," she said. "It'll be nice to finally have someone underneath me."

"You go, girl," a passing housemaid cracked. Craisy blushed crimson, and skittered away.

"Nice talk," a slick-haired footman said as he streaked by with a gleaming silver salver. "Farm-girls only have one thing on their minds."

"Except when it comes to you, Dhumbas," said another housemaid.

"Dhumbas, don't forget the bicarbonate of soda for the table." Mr. Cussin pounded his burning sternum. "Cook is in fine form this morning."

Another footman approached; in his wide Yorkshire palm were two small blue objects. "Mr. Cussin, her ladyship asked me to put out these salt-and-peppers instead of the silver ones. I think it's some American custom."

"Oh Lord." The butler regarded the pair of ceramic hats with unbridled distaste. "Who or what are the Chicago Cubs?"

The footman shrugged blandly — then he noticed me. "New tray-boy? Welcome to Downturn." We shook hands. "A word of advice: never try to carry one of Cook's soufflés on your own; the last fellow got crushed flat. Or was he the one that got burned up? No, he suffocated! Anyway, we go through tray-boys at a terrific rate." Anything I might say seemed likely to reveal the terror newly blossoming in my bowels, so I just smiled.

"Oh, I'm only

Pre-Downturn days at Ripping Foundling Home. That's me in the middle, with the pointed hat. From left: Clive, Nigel, Clive Two, Othello, me, Mal, Reg, I forget, Reg the Git.

chaffing you…You hope." Smiling, Killem turned to Mr. Cussin. "Doesn't talk much, does he?"

"If only the same could be said for the rest of you…" The butler handed back the little hats. "Put them out, Killem, monstrous as they might be." The footman walked away briskly, and Mr. Cussin sighed to no one in particular. "*Yanks*."

• • •

They fitted me for livery, and measured me for a coffin, in case it ever came to that, and within the hour, I was standing by Cola, Countess of Cantswim's bed, getting used to the weight of the tray. I think I dropped everything at least twice, but her ladyship was exceedingly kind. Except when it came to the St. Louis Cardinals, who or whatever they were. "Promise me you're not a fan of those horrible men, Percy."

"I promise, m'lady."

"Then we'll get along just fine."

The lady of the house liked to read the paper as she ate breakfast, and clip coupons. Lady Cantswim had been born rich, as the heiress to a Chicago soda pop fortune, and planned to stay that way. One of her bromides was "Never give anything away."

I learned them all, that first morning. M'lady had a mother's habit of instructing every child with whom she came into contact, and so my eight-year-old self triggered an endless stream of maxims. "Gin makes you mean," "Never freeze mayonnaise," *et cetera*. We were rounding out our first hour together when Lady Cantswim said absently, "Every great fortune is founded on a great crime, little Percy. That's why I call my husband 'Robber.'"

His lordship burst in as if conjured, brandishing two telegrams and giggling. Whatever the Earl's faults, he was uncommonly free with the servants (and not just the maids, either). He would sneeze, cough, even blink in front of us, just as if we were real people. Robber, Sixth Earl of Cantswim, truly had "the common touch."

"Cola, have you seen this morning's papers? I've just received the most hilarious telegrams. But you have to read them together to get the joke." His lordship handed over two squares of brown

paper for his wife to read.

"DEAR BORING OLD BOB
TITANIC IS AWESOME STOP
GOT LAST BERTH STOP
WHAT COULD POSSIBLY GO WRONG QUESTIONMARK
YOU ARE SOOO PWNED
COUSIN JERK."

April 1912 • Price: One Ha'penny

THE URCHIN.

Incorporating "Child Poverty."

BILL: Why are you crying? Don't you like cheese?
WILL: I am lactose-intolerant.

Parents—Are They Overrated? .... G. Nesbitt
I Made It; So Must You! .... A. Carnegie
Tiny Tim Was a Whiner .... P. Hetchworth
Fiction: "Hard But Fair" .... Mrs. J. Winthrop
God Loves the Poor, He Just Chooses
    Not To Show It .... Rev. R. Nesbitt
Gruel, Nature's Miracle Food .... E. Ponds

Win a trip to the HOSPITAL! Details inside!

"Now read the next one," his lordship said, barely able to contain himself.

"RMS TITANIC SUNK STOP
GREAT LOSS OF LIFE."

"Jerk changed his passage to make me feel like a country cousin then then…" The laughter began again, coming in great gusts. "What a git! What a stupendous, colossal knob!"

Her ladyship was not joining in. Silently, she put down the marmalade. "And did 'the knob' have his son with him?"

His lordship nodded in the affirmative, wiping away tears.

"Now Marry cannot marry him."

The Earl's laughter shut off like a cold-water tap. "Hadn't thought of that."

It was quiet. I coughed; uncomfortable silences give me post-nasal drip.

"Who's this, Typhoid Barry?"

"His name is Percy. He's our new tray-boy." Lady Cantswim sighed. "I suppose all that cold water was good for young Onan."

"Cola, that nickname is cruel and unfeeling. Two of my family are dead. Now is neither the time nor place to bring up a young boy's quirks."

"Honestly, Robber. It wasn't a quirk, it was a compulsion. His last visit, your mother caught him fondling some art…Did you at least take out life insurance on them, as I asked?"

"Certainly not!" the Earl said. "To profit on my heir's death, it's unspeakable—"

"No, it was to give Marry something to live on if he snuffed it, which is what happens every time you Cantswims get near water."

"Cola, I have scruples. "

"Then you can be the one to tell your eldest she's scru'ed."

• • •

Cool and immaculate, Lady Marry didn't so much walk as glide over the pea-gravel, as she and the Earl did a circuit of the grounds later that morning. I trailed after them, balancing a plate of sticks for the dog. The dog's name changed regularly, owing to his lordship's shaky grasp on reality, but he loved the animal dearly, so we pretended not to notice.

The canine gamboled friskily, jamming its wet snout into Lady Marry's unmentionables. "Careful, pup, I'm back on the market again…Papa, what's 'pwned' mean?"

"Some code, I expect. Those dot-dash chaps have a word for everything."

She spotted a piece of gravel slightly larger in circumference than all the others, and made a mental note to inform Mr. Cussin. "I understand black for mourning, but why must we all wear life-jackets?"

"Marry, two of our relations have drowned. We most certainly will wear life jackets."

"But we're in no danger."

"That's what *they* thought!"

• • •

I soon discovered that I wasn't the only new servant starting at Downturn that day. Standing next to Mr. Cussin was a twinkle-eyed pear-shaped gentleman who winced painfully with every step… and yet oozed pure, unadulterated sex.

"Mr. Baits, this is Percy, our new tray-boy. Feel free to mistreat him."

"I'd never," Mr. Baits said, and I felt something very strange in the general region of my woolens. But before I could pledge my undying love, they were onto the rest of the staff.

Craisy scampered through, dodging a rolling-pin. "Craisy, you've met. And that voice you hear bellowing recriminations is Mrs. Phatore, our cook."

"*Phatore?* Poor woman." Mr. Baits flashed his common decency like other men flash a fat roll of bills. "I expect she was teased a lot, in school."

"School, nothing," Dhumbas quipped. "We tease her now."

"No reason you should. Phatore's a fine old Yorkshire name," Mr. Cussin said. "This is our first footman. First name Dhumbas, last name 'Borrow,' as in steal."

Eyes flashing, Dhumbas returned to his newspaper. I thought I heard him mumble something about "myocardial infarction."

Mr. Cussin paid no attention. "Dhumbas is thoroughly evil, God knows why we keep him. On the other hand, he's balanced by our second footman, Killem, who's pleasant and laudable…"

"…so you're expecting him to snuff it?" Mr. Baits asked.

"As tragically as possible," Killem answered with a smile.

"Good man," Mr. Baits said as they shook hands.

A woman in black lay with her head on the table, snoring gently. Then she said muzzily, "Oh, Earl, I don't think we should, not here, not while Lady Cantswim is just in the next room—"

"That's Mrs. Snughes, our housekeeper," Mr. Cussin whispered. "She talks in her sleep."

Dhumbas leaned down and slowly whispered in her ear, "Titty clamps." "Steady on," Mr. Baits said. "You'll poison her dreams."

"Just trying to give her a bit of excitement, Mr. Baits."

A woman with a face like the business-end of a shillelagh walked in. "Who's the gimp?"

"May I introduce his lordship's new valet. Mr. Baits, this is her ladyship's maid, Miss O'Lyin. Or, as I like to call her, 'Miss Fetal Alcohol Poisoning of 1877.'"

"Every fetus's got a right to take a drink if they want to. It's the law."

"Downstairs I'm the law, Miss O'Lyin, you'd do well to remember that. This is Gwon, our housemaid who embodies a changing society —"

"Someone's got to do it," Gwon said goodnaturedly.

"— and finally Wanna Snogg, your love interest."

The valet grinned. "I'd hoped there'd be one of those."

"Nice to meet you, Mr. Baits. I'm mousy-hot and ready for action."

"Don't get stuck on me, Wanna. I'm bad news."

"Whatever do you mean?" she asked, backing him towards a corner.

"I'm a mysterious man with a murky past—"

"Keep talking."

" — and a troubled soul. I take others' secrets to the grave, and constantly do noble things which get me into desperate trouble. Don't try to save me — "

"Rowr," Wanna had him against the wall now, and was fiddling with his tie.

"No!" Mr. Baits cried. "You must stay away! I'm a puzzle, a riddle you cannot solve, a deep dark mystery that will bring you only pain!"

The rest of the staff stood transfixed. After all, this was the kind of thing people paid half-acrown for, down in Ripping.

"Anyone mind terribly if I climb on top of this gentleman?"

Just as things were about to get good, there was a sharp knock on the door, and the Earl walked in. "Hope I'm not disturbing anything—"

"Awww!" the whole staff groaned.

Mrs. Snughes woke up. "Just resting my eyes!"

• • •

As the cook loaded my head up with afternoon tea, I overheard Killem reading from his lordship's paper.

"Says here the word 'MIRAGE' was painted on the iceberg."

Craisy was hauling in a fresh bucket of cooking suet; she paused. "Really?"

"Yeah, and there were two people standing on it, in black clothes, smoking cigarettes."

"Get a move on, girl!" Mrs. Phatore brayed. "No one related to you was on that boat!"

"That's my line," I mumbled to Mr. Baits. He smiled.

• • •

"Smooth move, McGonigall's Laxative Powder," Miss O'Lyin sneered.

LADY MARRY
in her full-body quilted kapok
life-preservation gown.

"Don't know what you mean," Dhumbas replied. "Went down easy as you please, just like we planned."

"And yet here we are, still among the peons." She struck a match off my cheek; so far, ashtray duty was the worst part of being a tray-boy. "What odds did the old valet give you?"

"Four millions to one," Dhumbas said, exhaling. "How was I to know he'd welch on the bet?"

"Skulking off in the middle of the night with all our money, that's a clue. And us going all the way to the North Pole with a bloody ice pick and a bucket of paint."

"Travel's broadening." Dhumbas ground out his cigarette. "Never you mind. One of my plans will pay off."

"Or they could sack you."

"They'd never, Miss O'Lyin. You neither. We're too important to the plot."

•   •   •

As Mr. Cussin always said, "A tray-boy in a great house sees all, hears all, and says nothing." When I was not actively serving the family, I would be standing behind a drape with only my shoes showing, ready to do whatever was asked.

For a few days, no one upstairs could bring themselves to discuss the issue at hand; the sudden break in the family line was too shocking, too awful, and as you'll see, at Downturn not saying important things was a way of life. Finally the Earl could take no more, and broached the topic one evening at dinner.

"There is an important issue that has arisen, something I'm sure each of you is thinking about, something that affects us all."

"Dad, you are totally right," Lady Unsybil said, whipping out a clipboard. "For too long, a free Tibet has — "

Her ladyship rolled her eyes. "Unsybil, I told you: no petitions at the table."

"But China's being totally harsh — "

"I don't see what business it is of ours," Lady Violent said. "Surely such matters are best left to the Tibetans."

"Granny, just because they're foreign — "

"Where ever does she get all these causes?" Lady Marry asked wearily.

"One of the Skelton boys," Lady Edict offered. "The one with the weird name who doesn't wash."

"Gramsci Bakunin Skelton is not a weird name!"

"Ow!" Lady Edict flushed. "Don't kick me under the table, bint!"

"Girls! No one is a bint!" her ladyship declared. "We can discuss the eccentricities of the Skeltons another time."

As his children squabbled and his wife refereed, the Earl felt his authority slipping away—almost as if it were happening not merely to him, at this table this one time, but to all people of his class, throughout society as a whole, forever. Yet he persevered. "The issue before us is: What are we to do about Marry?"

"Marriage is all she is good for," Lady Edict said. "She's practi-

cally labelled."

"Yes, as if you were named 'Virginia.'"

Lady Unsybil snickered quietly, "*Awesome.*"

The Dowager Countess shifted in her seat. "I would be much less concerned, if Marry had a sweeter disposition. How does she expect to be married if she's so indefatigably stroppy?"

"Get knotted, Granny."

"See what I mean?"

"*Your* mother managed somehow," Lady Cantswim said. "Robber, explain again why Marry can't inherit?"

"It all comes down to primogeniture. From the Italian, I believe…"

"You see, Unsybil?" cried Lady Violent. "See what caring about foreigners gets you?"

"They're in the world, Granny."

"A divine oversight. Which the Empire is slowly correcting."

His lordship plowed on through the crosstalk. "… *Primo*, meaning first or best, and *genital*, meaning —"

Lady Edict's pale face brightened with sudden understanding. "So the first baby with the right set of bits, hits the jackpot."

"*Certamente.*"

Lady Marry pushed back from the table defensively. "Nobody's fiddling with my bits, I can promise you that!" Lady Edict smirked. "Oh Marry, everyone's fiddled with your bits."

His lordship frowned; his wife and daughters seemed to speak their own private language, like the dot-dash chaps. "What do you mean, Edict, everyone's fiddled with Marry? Cola, what does she mean?"

"Nothing, dear. Just sibling rivalry."

"Tell that to Papa's old valet," Lady Edict snorted.

Lady Violent felt the conversation veering towards the modern, so she placed her fingers in her ears and hummed.

"I always wondered why he left in the middle of the night," Lady Unsybil said.

"Naked," Lady Edict added gleefully. "*Sobbing.*"

Lady Cantswin and Lady Marry looked over at Mr. Cussin frantically. Hint received the butler rumbled, "I believe it's time for pudding."

•   •   •

By the end of that week, I had settled into the rhythms of daily life at Downturn Abbey. I was still undiscovered, and no great personages had stopped by, unless you wished to include two ladies hawking subscriptions to *Lo! The Journal of What Will Be*. But it was a pleasant place, where one could tell whom to befriend or avoid by how much they smoked. I was strangely drawn to Mr. Baits — as everyone was, even the Earl's dog — but I never felt I knew him. He kept himself to himself, which I suppose was a great part of his charm. There was a lot of exposition in that household.

Drawing made by crewmember of the Carpathia, April 1912.

I never could tell what was wrong with the valet, why he winced with every step, why there was a slight clanking in the vicinity of his gentleman's spigot. As a lowly tray-boy, I never had the courage to ask. However, I was passing through the corridor outside the servants' hall when someone else did.

"Well, well," said Dhumbas. "If it isn't old Master Baits."

"It's not the low humor I mind," Mr. Baits said, "it's the historical anachronism."

"Then you're in for a long book." The evil first footman crowded the heartthrob. "If you'd ever like to have a go, I'd be happy to accommodate you."

"Somehow I don't think you're talking about fighting."

"That's just the thing—you won't know until it's too late. Some dark night, I'll come from behind—"

"There are children present, Dhumbas. I'm warning you."

"You don't look so tough to me."

"Appearances can be deceiving. You know the Boer War? I ended that."

"Aren't you the hard man? Let's see if you're all talk." Dhumbas reached down—then pulled his hand away as quick as if he'd been burned. "'Struth! What're you wearing down there? Armor?"

"As I've said, there are children present. Come along, Percy." And with the mystery no closer to being solved, Mr. Baits took my hand and we walked out.

• • •

It took only a telegram to the International Lavender Conspiracy for the Duke of Crowbar to learn of Lady Marry's changed circumstances, and one day soon at luncheon, Lady Cantswim announced brightly that the Duke was coming for a visit.

His lordship, however, was not so cheered. "I wouldn't get your hopes up, Marry."

"Why not?" Lady Cantswim asked. "With a new dress, a Wondercorset—"

"Crowbar's a nickname," her husband interrupted. "From boarding school. Let's leave it at that."

"Where did he attend?" Lady Violent asked.

"Beton."

"Oh, I see. That explains everything." When her American daughter-in-law still did not comprehend, the Dowager Countess spelled it out. "Do you know how they separate the men from the boys at Beton? With a crowbar,"

Lady Marry and Lady Edict sniggered loudly; their sister didn't. "Can I just

say? This society is totally heteronormative."

"Oh, you English and your old school rivalries," Lady Cantswim said lightly. She patted Lady Marry's hand. "Our daughter's more than a match for a little fabulousness, aren't you, Marry?"

• • •

Of course Lady Marry wasn't a match for the Duke's fabulousness; no woman was. After a dreadful evening spent discussing whether all the statuary in Downturn "mightn't look frightfully better with all those awful breasts and hips fixed," Lady Marry went upstairs to lick her wounds and curse her wrong bits. I, on the other hand, was dispatched to the Duke's room, for any nocturnal tray needs.

When I got to the Duke's door, I heard the sounds of a heated discussion, so I stayed outside.

"Who would believe you, a lowly footman?" His Grace was saying. "A Duke, DJ'ing at a club in Manchester? The very idea is preposterous."

"But I have *proof!*" I recognized this voice as Dhumbas's. Discretion told me to walk on, but my affection for Mr. Baits was stronger. I squatted down at the keyhole to have a better look.

"Proof? Are you speaking of these?" The Duke brandished a handful of club flyers.

"Give 'em over!" As Dhumbas lunged, His Grace tossed the incriminating cardstock into the fire. The Duke held Dhumbas back, as the glossy paper burned and the flames flashed colors. "Sorry, chum. 'DJ Crowbar' must remain our little secret."

Dhumbas shook himself free. "I'll get you for this," he seethed. "I want my 12-inches back!"

"As usual, you overestimate yourself." His Grace smiled cruelly. "Oh — you meant your LPs. I'll see if I can find them…Anyway, we'll always have Eighties Night."

Wearing a look of pure murder, Dhumbas thundered towards the door. I turned and scurried down the corridor just in time.

• • •

The entire household, upstairs and down, was dismayed over the Duke's hasty departure. "He even insulted my salt-and-pepper shakers," Lady Cantswim said.

"I don't think we can put it off any longer," the Earl said. "I am going to write my second cousin, Dratyew Crawly."

"So you won't fight for your daughter?"

"My dear, if this were a legal procedural I'd consider it, but as ITV ordered a costume drama, I think you had better reconcile yourself."

"Promise me one thing — " Lady Cantswim caught the Earl's arm as he headed for the library. "Make him *swear* he's not into dudes." **B**

A CLUB FLYER
I found under the Duke's bed.

Noah and the Dinosaurs

A lot of people, some of whom are in charge of big powerful countries, religious organizations and voting blocs, think these are the end times. They are jiggling their legs and tapping their fingers as they wait impatiently for holy men to come back from the dead or rise up out of a well. But whether our species is heading toward a permanent state of delusion, anxiety or imminent disaster, we can all learn something about survival in difficult times by examining the heroic story of Noah and the Ark.

Here was a man unbothered by daunting tasks starting with day one when he had to find enough gopher wood to build a boat 300 cubits by 50 cubits by 30 cubits while at the same time figuring out what gopher wood and cubits even were. And that was well before he sunk into the chaos of rounding up two of every ordinary species of animal — many of which were the natural enemies of each other, and therefore programmed toward mayhem or flight. Weasels and spiny echidnas are just two examples of thousands of animals that don't necessarily come when they were called.

So things were very complicated from the get-go… even before God threw in: "Of every *clean* beast thou shalt take to thee by sevens, the male and his female: and of beasts that are *not clean* by two, the male and his female." [Italics mine, not His.] That meant that once Noah managed to figure out which of his potential passengers qualified as sufficiently "clean", he had to go out and find fourteen of them, not two. Fortunately for Noah the departure arrangements were so last-minute that a lot of the beasts in question didn't have the time to bathe.

At that point Noah's workday was only beginning. According to The Creation Museum in Kentucky, he then had to figure out how to gather two of every species of dinosaur.

No, dinosaurs are not specifically mentioned in Genesis. But The Creation Museum points out that since the Earth is 6,000 years old, and God requested "every living thing that is with thee, of all flesh, both of fowl, and of cattle, and of every creeping thing that creepeth upon the earth," dinosaurs qualified. They creepethed as much as anyone.

For Noah, the extra burden of adding seven hundred species of dinosaurs into the already problematic mix had to be almost incalculable. Especially when you stop to ponder that many of them lived 183 million years apart from each other! So imagine how Noah must have felt as he was in the middle of successfully rounding up two 20-foot-high Tyrannosaurus Rexes, only to discover that he couldn't also bag a couple of Triceratops because they lived 25 million years away.

"How much craziness is one six-hundred-year-old man expected to handle?" Noah must have thought. "Like I didn't already have my hands full, keeping the hyenas and the deer away from each other!"

But let's be honest: When you're making travel plans for 1,400 dinosaurs, you no sooner solve one problem then you've created another one. It's hard enough to steer an ark through a life-threatening catastrophic storm without having to figure out how to see past two velociraptors!

"Maybe if I move the larger herbivores like the brontosaurus down to the first level, I can cut holes in the upper deck so they can stick their giant heads out to breathe," he may have woken up in the middle of the night deliberating, after it occurred to him that if he didn't place the giant lizards correctly, he would cause the ship to list.

continued ☛

············ ◆ ············

Merrill Markoe *has published eight books and written for a long list of television shows and publications, including the one you are holding.*

ETIENNE DELESSERT

"I guess if I tranquilized them and stacked them in a pyramid toward the center of the Ark, that might fix the ballast problem while also cutting down on trampled mice and rabbits!"

And the less said about dinosaur dung, the better. The enormity of trying to clean up after only a few dinosaurs, let alone 1,400, would have been taxing even for Noah's three younger sons, who were only in their 500s. Assuming they, like so many men of legend, married much younger women, it's still difficult to know what kind of cooperation could be expected from a group of exhausted seagoing trophy wives in their two hundreds. And that's if we presuppose that they were reasonably good sports.

But even if Noah somehow managed to get the dinosaurs under control, think how much more there was to do! He still had to divvy up the 15,000 cubits among 150,000 pairs of mammals, 2 million pairs of insects and 9,000 species of birds, all requiring their own special menus and toilet areas. When God casually threw in the edict that "the fowls of the air" be brought in "by sevens, the male and the female; to keep seed alive upon the face of all the earth", I wonder if it even occurred to Him that Noah would practically need a separate smaller ark just to store the seed and mealworms required for 126,000 birds.

"The jackals alone will need 64 pounds of wildebeest each, times 40 days. Where am I going to get 2,560 pounds of wildebeest?" must have been one of thousands of food-supply questions racing around in his head while he pulled out his hair at 3 A.M. "That's at one meal a day. And good luck with that because if I know jackals, they want to eat when they want to eat, period. Don't even get me started on sauropods."

Those forty days and forty nights must have felt interminable.

Of course God being God, he had a few more final addenda: "Bring forth with thee every living thing that is with thee, of all flesh, both of fowl, and of cattle, and of every creeping thing that creepeth upon the earth." Easy for God to say, but that meant 600-year-old Noah and his 500-year-old sons and their 200+-year-old wives had to figure out how to escort all the rhinoceri and potato bugs and blue-footed boobies and weasels and pangolins and spiders in addition to all the dinosaurs safely down a plank without incident, aware that any stampeding might inadvertently wipe out an entire species.

At some point Noah must have turned to Mrs. Noah, inhaled deeply and said, "Honey, the next time God makes us an offer, no matter how much he sweet-talks me, just tie an anchor around my leg and let me drown, okay?"

On the bright side, hopefully everyone on board found some comfort in knowing that no matter where they landed, they would have their choice of vacant oceanfront property. **B**

THE WORST THING I EVER DID.

RICK GEARY '16

MY NEIGHBOR MINNIE "DROPPED BY" ONE MORNING.

BUT I JUST WASN'T UP FOR ANOTHER OF HER TEDIOUS VISITS.

I COULDN'T OPEN THAT DOOR... I JUST COULDN'T.

I DARED NOT EVEN MOVE.

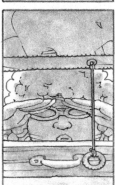

SHE WALKED AROUND THE HOUSE, PEERING THRU EVERY WINDOW.

FINALLY, SHE MUTTERED, "I KNOW YOU'RE THERE"...

AND WENT HOME.

I FELT TERRIBLE WHEN 3 DAYS LATER SHE WAS FLATTENED BY A STREETCAR.

SHE MUST HAVE TOLD PEOPLE ABOUT ME FOR I WAS BARRED FROM THE FUNERAL.

A DANCE TO FEIFFER
BY PETER KUPER

MEET MY FRIEND AND MENTOR, JULES FEIFFER...

BOY--THEY DON'T MAKE COMICS LIKE THEY USED TO!

A LIST OF HIS ACCOMPLISHMENTS BEGINS TO SOUND ABSURD! PULITZER, POLK, OBIES, OUTER CIRCLE CRITICS AWARDS...

CHRIST--THE GUY EVEN WON AN ACADEMY AWARD FOR HIS ANIMATED SHORT, MONRO!

IT'S ABOUT A FOUR YEAR-OLD WHO ACCIDENTALLY GETS DRAFTED

WHICH IS HOW I FELT WHEN THEY INDUCTED ME DURING THE KOREAN WAR!

AT 17 HE HAD THE MOXY TO APPROACH HIS HERO, CARTOONIST WILL EISNER--AND HE GOT HIRED!

INITIALLY HE JUST NEEDED A SYCOPHANT AROUND...

KNOCK KNOCK

WILL EISNER

BUT HE GAVE ME A SHOT AND I BECAME A WRITER!

FEIFFER WAS LIKE FORREST GUMP! IN HIS 20'S HE JUST HAPPENED TO BE NEIGHBORS WITH NORTON JUSTER...

SO DO YOU WANT TO ILLUSTRATE THE PHANTOM TOLLBOOTH, OR WHAT?!

...UM, OKAY!

JULES SHOWED UP AT THE OFFICES OF THE VILLAGE VOICE AND THEY GAVE HIM A SPOT THAT LASTED 40 YEARS!

THEY GAVE ME TOTAL FREEDOM, BUT NO PAY FOR THE FIRST EIGHT YEARS!

ALONG THE WAY HE BEGAN PENNING GROUND-BREAKING BOOKS, PLAYS AND SCREENPLAYS.

FIRST PEOPLE SAID MY COMIC STRIPS WERE LIKE PLAYS-- THEN THEY SAID MY PLAYS WERE LIKE COMIC STRIPS!

CLINK CLINK

WHEN WE MET IN THE 1980'S HE WAS ON THE VERGE OF REINVENTING HIMSELF YET AGAIN, THIS TIME AS A CHILDRENS' BOOK AUTHOR...

I WAS SICK AND TIRED OF BEING IGNORED BY JADED ADULTS, SO I DECIDED TO TRY AND REACH 'EM WHILE THEY WERE YOUNG!

MAN IN THE CEILING

THE LOST BEAR

WATCHING HIS CAREER ARC GAVE ME THE INSPIRATION TO EXPERIMENT AND EVOLVE IN MY OWN WORK...

HEY-- DO YOU MIND GIVIN' ME A LITTLE PRIVACY?!

SHAMELESS PLUG FOR MY NEW BOOK

WAIT!! WHAT'S THIS NEW INCARNATION?!

TA-DA!

I'M A GRAPHIC NOVELIST!

Kill My Mother

CRASH!

B-BUT HOW'S THIS POSSIBLE? YOU'RE EIGHTY-SIX!

EIGHT-SIX, SCHMEIGHTY-SIX!

YOU JUST GOTTA KEEP DANCIN' KID...

KEEP DANCIN'!

B

A Rendez-Vous with *The New Yorker*

Fresh from a family spat that doomed his college education,
Peter Arno *wagers his future on a fledging comic weekly.*

At age twenty-one, marinating in the nightlife of Prohibition-era Greenwich Village, the man who was to become Peter Arno had yet to make a dent in his father's town.

Tiring of doing illustrations for a silent film studio near Times Square, his thoughts drifted back to making a living playing music. In June of 1925, he was considering accepting an offer of five hundred dollars to regroup his jazz band and take it to Chicago. Before accepting, however, he decided to make one "final try" at selling his art.

A humor magazine calling itself *The New Yorker* had appeared on newsstands in February of that year. The magazine's art featured single panel cartoons and illustrations — an Arno specialty in college — and its

"Hey Jack, let's have another look at that map." Peter Arno in **The Yale Record***, 1923.*

covers were somewhat comic as well. If Curtis Peters had any possibility of making a living as a cartoonist, *The New Yorker* was his last, best hope.

The brainchild of Colorado-born Harold Ross, the publication was aimed at Arno's own cohort, the young, sophisticated post–World War I generation on vivid display in F. Scott Fitzgerald's 1920 novel, *This Side of Paradise*. Carrying the idea around for years, Ross was able to realize *The New Yorker* when he found financial backing from one of his card-playing pals, Fleischmann's Yeast scion Raoul Fleischmann. An inveterate gambler like so many in the Algonquin Round Table (the group had its own poker-playing auxiliary, nicknamed the "Thanatopsis Literary and Inside Straight Club"), Fleischmann was just the person to bet on a new magazine, a risky venture even in 1925. Nearly forty, Fleischmann was looking around for some way to relieve his boredom; after Ross set the idea of a weekly New York–centered comic magazine before him, Fleischmann was in.

Ross, with the assistance of his wife, newspaperwoman Jane Grant, worked feverishly on developing the first issue, something graphically resembling a cross between *Punch* and *Judge*; editorially, it exhibited a breezy, unremarkable, contemporary cheekiness. The cover art featured a puzzling drawing of a top-hatted fellow right out of the late 1800s. The magazine was greeted with a shrug; subsequent issues were met with similar indifference.

The New Yorker was located in a Fleischmann-owned building in a neighborhood familiar to Arno: West 45th Street — the same street and on the same side as Arno's old supperclub haunt, The Rendez-Vous. Arno gathered together some drawings, stuffed them "in a loosely tied sheath," then traveled uptown to West 45th Street to drop off his work. Wearing ragged sneakers and paint-smeared canvas pants, Arno showed up at the magazine and handed over his drawings to a young man — just two years older than Arno — named Philip Wylie. A few days later, Arno

.... ◆ ....

Michael Maslin's new biography, *Peter Arno: The Mad, Mad World of The New Yorker's Greatest Cartoonist,* is available everywhere.

received a call saying *The New Yorker* would like to buy one of his drawings.

Coming exactly two years to the month since he'd left Yale, this first published drawing (not in a school publication) was signed in script, "Arno." It appeared in a generous space, three columns wide, on page six of *The New Yorker*'s June 20, 1925 issue. Still, it was a drawing that wouldn't have been out of place in *The Yale Record* alongside his other non-captioned work.

Arno's first contribution was neither a cartoon, nor an illustration, but what *The New Yorker* referred to as a "spot." Although the magazine was only eighteen issues old at the time of Arno's arrival, it had already established graphic elements that would go on to appear in every issue hence; the spot was one of these elements. Spots are the drawings of trivets, flowerpots, bicycles, steam shovels, saltshakers, frogs, tennis racquets, et cetera, that have no connection to the text around them, but enliven and loosen the otherwise gray pages.

Arno's first drawing contained basic elements of his drawings yet to come: ironclad composition and dramatic use of black versus white. It portrays a woman and a top-hatted man in good humor, carrying a walking stick, crossing a city street at night under the gaze of two somewhat shady-looking men,

one looking at the couple and the other with his head down, leaning on a lamp post. There's a dramatic sweep to the scene, with front-lit buildings in perspective and grand shadows cast from the couple out on the town. It's an "us versus them" theme with not a little edge to it. It's possible the couple is in danger, but of course, we'll never know.

The spot is signed "Arno" in humble script that creeps up the lefthand side of the drawing. The days of signing his work "Curtis Peters" were over. Why he juggled his name — dropping his surname for a shortened version of his middle name, and stripping his last name, Peters, of its "s" and making it his new first name — was never documented. Legend has it that he did not want to embarrass his father the judge by using "Peters," but considering the bad blood between father and son, it's conceivable Arno wanted instead to disassociate himself from his namesake. Arno's New York Times obituary says he told friends he changed his name because "he wanted to separate his identity from his father's." As psychologically important as it might have been, this new signature in no way resembles the bold signature that anchored his later work.

Arno was a work in progress, as was *The New Yorker*, and they were

destined to blossom together. But was it love at first sight? Memories on this point are mixed. Ralph Ingersoll, the magazine's first managing editor, once told James Thurber that Arno's drawings "did not go over with the art meetings for the first few months, but were usually laughed at as being not very good or funny." Surprised, Thurber ran Ingersoll's story past Rea Irvin, the magazine's first art director. Irvin said, "I do not remember Arno's drawings ever being considered not good enough for *The New Yorker*. At least, Ross and I always liked them."

Irvin's recollection makes more sense; both Arno and Ross were groping for a new kind of humor, one that spoke to their generation, not the ones that came before. "In the days of the old *Life*, *Puck*, and *Judge*," Arno later wrote, "many an artist drew endless variations of his particular specialty — boy-and-girl, old-gentleman-and-small-boy, monkey-talking-to-giraffe — and then some bedevilled staffer would sit down and tack on whatever variation of stock joke, pun, or he-and-she dialogue he could think of."

Compare this to a memo from Ross to *New Yorker* artists, circulated in 1925: "We want drawings which portray or satirize a situation, drawings which tell a story. We want to record what is going on, to put down metropolitan life and we want this record to be based on fact—plausible situations with authentic backgrounds…Our attitude is one tending towards the humorous and the satirical. By humorous we do not mean comic stuff captioned by a 'wise-crack.'"

This was Ross's blueprint for what would come to be known as "*The New Yorker* Cartoon." It was more than just a label — it meant a host of things, not least of which was quality. Quality of design, of execution, of captions perfectly and seemingly effortlessly synchronized with the art. In 1925, the popular magazines were still running cartoons whose goal was to produce a giggle. Arno's *New Yorker* work, and the work eventually produced by his fellow *New Yorker* cartoonists, broke from the norm — their cartoons lingered beyond the belly laugh. Simple as it may sound, Ross's insistence on

SPARKS

a *New Yorker* "attitude" resulted in the readership finally finding cartoons they could relate to, a type of humor, Arno later wrote, that "related to everyday life; believable, based on carefully thought-out, integrated situations, with pictures and captions interdependent. This interdependence was the most important element of the cartoon." From the beginning, Arno and Ross were pulling in the same direction.

The *New Yorker* that opened its doors to Arno was, in those first months of life, a remarkably slim operation. The art department consisted of one part-time employee: Irvin. Irvin's career had been in full swing before Ross hired him; the one-time cartoonist and actor was art editor with the humor magazine *Life* before Ross wooed him to work at *The New Yorker*. Thurber himself credited Irvin with the success of all things art-related at the dawn of the magazine: "Rea Irvin did more to develop the style and excellence of *New Yorker* drawings and covers than anyone else, and was the main and shining reason that the magazine's comic art in the first two years was far superior to its humorous prose."

As early as June of 1925, *The New Yorker* had begun to build a stable of regular contributing artists, among them Irvin, Reginald Marsh, Miguel Covarrubias, Gardner Rea, Al Frueh, Alice Harvey, John Held Jr., and Ralph Barton. Yet despite all the talent in place during the magazine's first six months, the only artist regularly matching Ross's ideal was Helen Hokinson. Hokinson's gentle ink-and-gray-wash drawings welcomed the reader into her world of comfortable scenarios; of people, usually women, set in friendly situations or engaged in friendly activities such as shopping, dining out, attending dance classes, visiting art museums, attending the opera or dog shows.

Arno's work — his world — shared some of Hokinson's scenarios (restaurants and the opera, for instance). But it was an edgier place than Hokinson's — less comfortable, slightly dark. Threaded throughout Arno's world was the implication that something unsavory was about to take place, or

just had. Arno's rascally nature was the perfect compliment to Hokinson's gentler wit.

With the addition of Arno to *The New Yorker* — and in 1926, the sudden explosion of his work in the magazine — Ross had his magnetic opposites: Arno and Hokinson, pulling in a much-needed readership.

Following his entry to *The New Yorker* in June, Arno's contributions continued to be spot drawings, not cartoons. Finally, in the October 3 issue, *The New Yorker* published its first Arno cartoon. His "amazing luck" had finally begun, and nothing would be the same after that — not Arno, not *The New Yorker*, and not America itself. ◗

THE DREW FRIEDMAN
LIBRARY FROM FANTAGRAPHICS BOOKS

"I'm grateful to Drew Friedman for every new piece in his vast, riveting panorama of the jacked-up, hellbent american spectacle: comic and horrific, loving and appalled, obsessive and devil-may-care, brilliant and vulgar, familiar and uncanny. He's our own William Hogarth and Thomas Rowlandson and George Grosz all wrapped into one."
— *Kurt Anderson, host of NPR's Studio 360*

"Drew Friedman isn't just a brilliant artist. He makes you smell the stale cigarettes and cold brisket and you say, thank you for the pleasure." — *Sarah Silverman*

"I love Drew Friedman. He's my favorite artist."
— *Howard Stern*

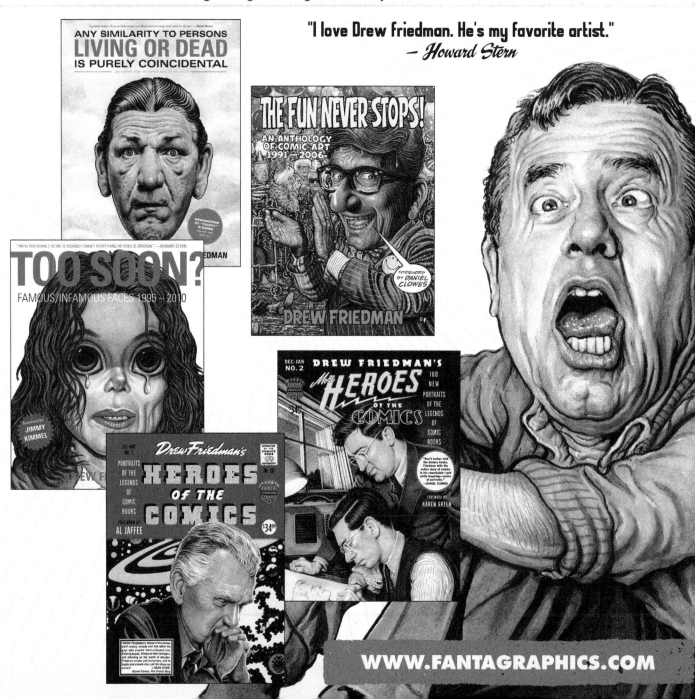

BY J.A. WEINSTEIN (@JohnnyStyne)

LOVE AND MERCY 2

In which John Cusack rips a hole in the time/space continuum

Love & Mercy is a 2014 biopic about Brian Wilson (b. 1942) of The Beach Boys. In the film, actor John Cusack (b. 1966) portrays Wilson in the year 1988.

This, then, is an imagined late night phone call between John Cusack and Brian Wilson of The Beach Boys.

CUSACK: Brian, it's Q.
WILSON: My brother.
CUSACK: You awake?
WILSON: Am I dreaming?
CUSACK: Right.
WILSON: Man, after *Love & Mercy*, when I hear your voice now, I think 1988 me. You did such a good job playing 1988 me.
CUSACK: That's why I'm calling, my brother.
WILSON: It's been great talking to you.
CUSACK: Wait. Don't hang up. Brian!
CLICK.
CUSACK calls back.
WILSON: I just dreamed you called me.
CUSACK: I dreamed you hung up on me.
WILSON: Oh. My. God.
CUSACK: Let's go back into our dream, Brian.
WILSON: Okay, I'm back.
CUSACK: Right. It was so kickass playing 1988 you in *Love & Mercy*. It was such an overwhelmingly amazing opportunity and I want to return the favor, man.
WILSON: You want me to play 1988 you? *Say Anything* you? *(crying)* I'd have to brush up on my kickboxing.
CUSACK: Brian, what I offer you is better than playing *Say Anything* me.
WILSON: *(sniffles)* Better? How? HOW?!
CUSACK: In the year 2014, I played 1988 you. I was 48.
WILSON: Okay.
CUSACK: Today, in 2016, you are 74. Do you know what year I will be 74?
WILSON: Uh, no.
CUSACK: I will be 74 in 2040.
SILENCE.
CUSACK: My vision is a documentary set 24 years in the future, in 2040, when I will be 74, that takes a backward glance on the 2014 making of *Love & Mercy*.
WILSON: Am I in it? The vision?
CUSACK: Yes. In my vision, 2016 you plays 2040 me, reminiscing about 2014 me, playing 1988 you.
WILSON: I, as 2040 you, would talk about 2014 you playing 1988 me?
CUSACK: Exactly.

WILSON: How old will I be?
CUSACK: 74.
WILSON: I'm 74 now. How can I be 74 in the future?
CUSACK: You won't be 74 in the future.
WILSON: What?
CUSACK: *I'll* be 74 in the future. You'll be playing me at 74 in the future.
WILSON: Who am I playing?
CUSACK: 2040 me.
WILSON: You want me to play you who played me 52 years ago?
CUSACK: What?
WILSON: In 2040, 1988 is 52 years ago.
CUSACK: *(beat)* THAT IS EXACTLY RIGHT!
WILSON: Then, brother, I'll do it.
CUSACK: This is so incredibly awesome. I'll have my people get in touch with your people.
WILSON: Not 1988 me's people though. 1988 me's people was kind of an asshole.
CUSACK: Tell 2014 me about it! That's why we're going 2016 all the way. Both sides!
WILSON: Thanks, brother.
CUSACK: Is there anything you want in your dressing room?
WILSON: Gee…1974 me wants a sandbox.
CUSACK: Already done. Remember, 2014 me researched 1974 you to prepare to play 1988 you.
WILSON: So what does 1974 you want in my dressing room?
CUSACK: 1974 me was eight, so — the pitcher's mound from Wrigley Field.
WILSON: To fill the sandbox! Perfect harmony, Q!
CUSACK: I'm incredibly stoked for this.
WILSON: Totally. 2016 me can't wait to play 2040 you remembering 2014 you researching 1974 me to play 1988 me.
CUSACK: In 2016 you's dressing room, on the pitcher's mound, dressed as 1974 me!
WILSON: Yeah!
CUSACK: 2016 me's writing a note to 2016 me: "1974 Cubs jersey for 2016 Brian. Boys small."
WILSON: 2016 me's so psyched to wear that! 1988 me's people would never let me wear that! But 2016 me's gotta be me, Q. At all times.
CUSACK: Me, too!
WILSON: See ya in 2040, Q.
CUSACK: See ya, my brother.
WILSON: *(pause)* Wait. Can I ask you a question?
CUSACK: Anything, Brian.
WILSON: Am I awake?

B

J.A. WEINSTEIN *(@JohnnyStyne) conceived "This Day In Hasselhoff History" for* **The Daily Show.** *This piece marks J.A.'s "return to comedy after thirteen years of marriage."*

BY BRIAN McCONNACHIE

A LETTER TO THE COMMISH

Never show the body of a drowned running back

Dear Roger:

What a delight meeting you at Denise's wedding.

I hope the new season has been a bit more fun for you than the last couple. I don't know if you were serious when you asked me if I had any ideas — maybe that was the open bar talking! — but if you're still in the market for brainstorms, I think I've got one.

If I correctly recall, you said the NFL's two biggest areas of concern are fatal concussions and female fans. Well, this little innovation should put every mother's worries to rest — but lose none of the excitement of abnormally strong men running at and from one another.

The players who have been murdering people in bars and elevators is a conversation for another day.

Here's the big picture: Instead of football cleats, the players will wear swim fins on their feet and they'll play the entire game in a foot and a half of water.

That's all there is to it. It's that simple and that's why no one has thought of it before. It's been right under our noses the whole time.

They'll galumph about throwing and catching and tackling each other while splashing away. Probably even some out-and-out laughing may ensue as the players pay witness to their own happy antics.

Then, when the defense least expects it — here's the bonus: Are you ready? — somebody does a "quick kick." Who wouldn't want to see someone in swim fins try and kick a football while standing in a foot and a half of water? The place will go berserk. The stadium announcer will have to tell the fans to please, in the name of God, calm down or the stadium will start to collapse.

What mother wouldn't want to see her son have some wholesome play in this version of professional football? What NFL coach could be more sincere when he tells his players, "...now get out there today and have some fun?"

But remember, it's still NFL football, except for the swim fins and the foot and a half of water. The fans will love it. The players and

their mothers can, at last, start waving so-long to all that baffling brain damage.

But what if, you ask, a running back goes splashing up the middle, gets tackled and the whole defense piles on and won't get off and the runner is drowned?

What do you say to his mother?

Well first off, you're not going to say anything to anybody's mother because nothing like that will ever happen. NFL players wouldn't do that. Drowning the running backs is not in the culture.

But just in case, I've drawn up a contingency plan. I'm throwing this in for free, because I really want to see this happen.

How to Behave in the Unlikely Event of a Drowning.

First, never show the body of a drowned player. You go right to commercial. Then quickly get the drowned player off the field by forming a sort of huddle around the body and then, with quick, little shuffle steps, head for the sidelines and start looking for a big box. Then, wait about two to three days, no sooner, so as not to alarm anyone. Then you visit the mother. Maybe bring two NFL vice presidents and a former player who brings along his Super Bowl ring and lets her wear it while they comfort her.

Continuing with this enormous unlikelihood, the mother now has to realize, accidents happen. Give her a lot of stats on how common drowning really is. The "hidden truth about drowning," sort of thing. The "silent killer from beneath the sea and beyond," that's nobody's fault.

So, getting back to the game, will the referees be wearing swim fins as well, you may ask?

No. They can wear their street shoes until the league decides what's the best thing to do here. Saddle shoes are always a stylish statement. Brogans might fill the bill. Just before the start of the second half, a ref should hold up one of his feet and show off his handsome wet shoe to the camera. An honest, human-interest moment. Plus, some women love

anything to do with shoes.

I know that you know what all this says: It says some real life with normal people is going on here. How refreshing is that?

But back to the drowning. What about the so-called "criminal element"?

Again, there won't be any drownings! (Isn't that becoming clear by now?) Do you think for a moment the NFL is going to all the trouble of training athletes to run around in swim fins in a foot and a half of water, only to have a few bad apples jeopardize the whole operation?

Look who I'm asking. Will there be some pushback? Sure. But nothing we can't handle.

Roger, you more than anybody know you don't get to be the NFL in this life by neglecting the little things. There are still some matters, both big and small, to be decided. Do we use fresh water or salt? We tried using Gatorade, unfortunately it came off looking like urine. Beer's a natural, but that's a slippery slope to fall down; drunkenness and dare I say it, ACCIDENTAL drowning.

But this new football is coming, Roger. Coming to change the culture. Moms will be cheering. Players will be remembering where they parked their cars. Fans will be chanting, "More quick kicks!"

It's time to swim fin-up and make this magic happen.

Sincerely,
Brian McConnachie

P.S. — Here are some new football markets and safer, less aggressive names you might also want to consider:

The Saratoga Springs Philips Head Screw Drivers
The San Antonio Jumping Beans
The Hubba Hubba Tool and Dye Works
The Lakeview Paint Cans
The Florida Nap Time Boys
The Bricktown Clean Underpants Gang

...and I'm still working on some more. I'll keep in touch. — *B Mc.*

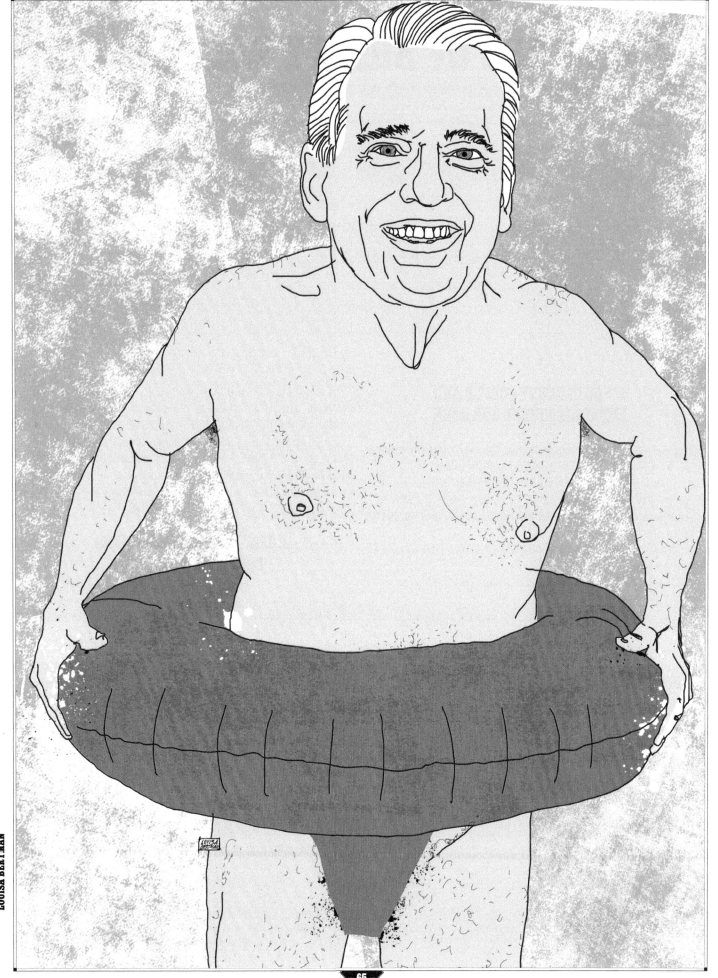

BY BEN ORLIN

THE TREE OF SHITTY WISDOM

In the sacred green of the deepest woods is a tree with no fucking clue

I. THE ELDERLY COUPLE AND THE UNGRATEFUL CHILDREN

An elderly couple stood before the tree. Warm sunlight filtered through the emerald quilt of leaves.

"O ancient Tree," they said, "our children refuse our way of life. To them, honor is a trinket, duty a burden, and tradition an arduous path leading nowhere. How can we guide them back to the light?"

"Sometimes," the tree replied, "to break with tradition is the only way to honor it."

The husband and wife looked at one another.

"The customs of a people are like the haircuts of aging men," continued the tree. "They change abruptly every few months, and in some cases vanish altogether." The tree paused. "But they are never forgotten."

"Perhaps that is so," said the husband, his brow darkening, "but how can we ensure that our children embrace our people's ways?"

"Never force words into the ear of a child, any more than you would force food into the mouth of the dog," spoke the tree. "Instead, speak softly into the dog's mouth, and place its food in your children's ears."

"Is it just me," the husband whispered, "or...?"

"Not just you," the wife whispered back.

"I'm sorry, do you have another question?" the tree asked.

"Your wisdom eludes us," the old woman said. "How can we make our children obey?"

"If a child counts too high, we must cut off a finger," said the tree. "And if a child does not count high enough, then we must lend him his brother's fingers for the afternoon."

The elderly couple left, grumbling. Later, they reflected that even their old age left them like mere children before the ancient figure of the tree. And thus, at last, they understood something of their children's rebelliousness.

II. THE BAFFLED PRINCE AND THE MAIDENS THREE

There came before the tree a young prince. He stood listening to the branches as they rustled with the brittle music of the wind.

"O beautiful Tree," he said, "I must wed before the summer ends. But I know not whom to marry. One girl is fair and clever, but not kind. The other is fair and kind, but not clever. And the last is fair and clever and kind, but not rich. Whom shall I choose?"

"Try as it might, love can never be like a wolf," said the tree. "For it has no teeth, it does not howl, and its urine marks no territory."

"Be that as it may," said the prince, trying not to think about what "love's urine" might refer to, "I love all three. How am I to know which love shall endure?"

"The future never speaks to the past," said the tree. "It remains as silent as a husband to a wife, as invisible as a

BEN ORLIN *is, surprisingly, a math teacher. His writing has appeared in* **The Atlantic, Slate, The Los Angeles Times,** *and elsewhere. His blog is* **Math with Bad Drawings** *(www.mathwithbaddrawings.com).*

frog to a butterfly."

The prince was confused. "But husbands do talk to wives, don't they?"

"The words we speak are autumn leaves that fall from the branch," said the tree. "And the words spoken back to us are spring leaves glued back onto the branch again."

"I don't think that's how leaves work," said the prince.

"Every memory is a wedding between yesterday and today," said the tree, "and every wish is a wedding between today and tomorrow."

"So 'today' is a bigamist?"

A soft wind shook the highest leaves of the tree, scattering unseen clouds of pollen towards the soft ground of the sacred forest.

"Yes."

The tree spoke no more to him after that. Eventually the prince went home and married the girl who was fair and kind, but not clever. They loved each other until they died, although she bored him occasionally.

III. THE POOR YOUNG GIRL

A girl came to the tree, seeking advice. Her eyes traced the grooves that ran like the threads of history across the tree's bark.

"O noble Tree," she said, "my father is gravely ill. How can I heal him?"

"There is no sickness in the mind except cruelty," said the tree, "and no cruelty in the body except sickness."

The girl nodded.

"And there is no sickness in the cruelty except mind," the tree continued, "and no body in the body except body."

The girl frowned. "I see?"

"You cannot see, for there is no such thing as sight," the tree said, "except for the eye's ability to perceive color, form, and contrast. Aside from that, there is no sight."

"Oh."

"Also, there is no such thing as hearing," the tree said. The girl waited for it to continue, but it seemed the tree had finished this particular thought.

"How, then, can I heal my father?" she asked.

"The healthy cannot heal the sick, any more than the land can dry the ocean."

"Then who can dry the ocean?"

"Fish," the tree said.

The girl sighed. "So how do I heal my father?"

"Laughter is the best medicine," said the tree. "Similarly, anger is the best soap, confusion is the hottest spice, and nepotism is nature's desk organizer."

The girl kicked an acorn at the tree, and trudged off to buy more Tylenol for her father, resolving never to seek professional advice on anything ever again. B

THE MAN WITH THE HOMBURG HAT

PROVIDENCE, R.I., ONE WINTER NIGHT IN 1983, AT THE CORNER OF ANGELL AND PROSPECT STREETS...

RETURNING TO MY DORM ROOM AFTER A LATE NIGHT SNACK, I SEE AN ELDERLY MAN WITH A HUNCHBACK WALKING GINGERLY THROUGH THE SNOW. HE WEARS A HOMBURG HAT AND CARRIES A BRIEFCASE. HIS DEMEANOR SUGGESTS TO ME THAT HE IS GOING TO WORK AS HE DESCENDS THE STEEP HILL TOWARDS THE CENTER OF TOWN. IT IS NEARLY MIDNIGHT.

OVER THE YEARS I SEE THE MAN AGAIN, SEVERAL TIMES. HE ALWAYS WEARS HIS HOMBURG HAT, CARRIES HIS BRIEFCASE, AND IS ALWAYS DESCENDING THE SAME HILL LATE AT NIGHT. TO SATISFY MY CURIOSITY, I INVENT PERSONALITIES FOR HIM: HE IS THE NIGHT EDITOR AT THE PROVIDENCE JOURNAL. HE IS A DOCTOR MAKING A HOUSE CALL. HE IS A RECLUSE AND THE WEALTHIEST MAN IN PROVIDENCE.

BY MICHAEL THORNTON

MY DINNER WITH ENNUI

Ten tips for dinner parties, in case you haven't given up

Dinner parties, like taxes and colonoscopies, are an inescapable part of adulthood. Even if you live in a doomsday bunker, the day will come when Marybeth wants to introduce you to her imaginary boss at the Secondary Ventilation Shafts 'R Us.

Dinner parties can end in satisfied back-patting between you and your partner, or a visit from the local hook and ladder company; the difference is planning and Xanax, but mostly planning. The following is everything you need to know for a successful night of stilted conversation.

1. **Aim to be hospitable, rather than impressive.** Impressing your guests is nice, but it's more important they feel welcome, never intimidated. By all means mix up a batch of martinis and serve $50/lb salumi made from pigs raised on Spanish hazelnuts and the films of Ingmar Bergman, however, if a man wants a beer with the $30 sandwich he's just assembled from your cheeseboard and the packet of mustard conjured from his breast pocket, hand the man a Schlitz.

2. **Alcohol should always be available.** Depending on your anxiety level, start the night by pouring one for yourself to consume in the pantry with the door closed while silently cursing your gluten intolerant friends and the ghost of Julia Child. When guests first arrive, offer them a cocktail, wine, or beer. Wine should be served throughout dinner (unless it's casual, like tacos), and after-dinner drinks should be on hand during and after dessert. Additionally, have plenty of sparkling water, ice, and one or two non-alcoholic options. If a guest drops a glass and then loudly exclaims, "Well at least it was empty!" get to pouring.

3. **Cook what you know.** A dinner party is not the time to take a crack at Thomas Keller's salmon cornets. It is the time to make your classics. However, if your 'classic' is ramen with a side of *Unbreakable Kimmy Schmidt*, make your mom's classics. Preferably select a meal that doesn't require much work once your guests arrive; roasts, casseroles, stews, soups, and anything you can make in a slow cooker are good options. You want to feel confident in predicting how your meal will taste, how long it will take, and that you won't end up serving twenty-five to life if your partner asks "How are things coming along?" If guests are at the door and dinner is a mess, try walking up the stairs backwards while holding a mirror and chanting "Rachael Ray."

4. **Set up the night before.** Clean the house, set the table, and make sure you have enough ice (you don't). An hour before your guests arrive is not the time to figure out the age of that diet tonic. If you have the time, a seasonally appropriate centerpiece will help to tie the table together — just keep it simple. Half of elegance is the appearance of effortlessness. A bowl of apples suggests fall; a papier-mâché Mayflower suggests you're in a book club with your cat.

5. **Don't make your guests take off their shoes.** This is the single biggest reason not to move to California. If you insist guests remove their shoes because you are intolerable and also awful, you better supply some slippers. Speaking personally, if God wanted me to be barefoot he would have made me that way, but I came into this world wearing a pair of Alden tassel loafers and I ask you to respect that fact.

6. **Keep the music going.** Music sets the mood and subconsciously defines how others see you. Buena Vista Social Club says, "I like to travel," Dave Brubeck says, "I'm white," and Nina Simone says "I'm white, but voted for Obama." Whatever you choose, keep the volume low, and keep the music playing — few things are more uncomfortable than true silence in the middle of a group dinner. You needn't fill every second with conversation, but the soundtrack should never be the melodious sounds of chewing, even if that is my favorite Philip Glass piece. Lastly, be careful of the repeat function. The second go around of "Leaving on a Jet Plane" says, "I'm stuck in the '60s." The sixth says, "Bush did 9/11."

7. **Facilitate the conversation.** Steer guests away from discussing their dreams, triathlon training, or the route they took to your house. Religion and politics are fine. When guiding conversation think about books you've recently read, a provocative news story, or ask about guests' future travel plans. If someone starts to share what it is like to sleep with a CPAP machine, interrupt and serve dessert.

8. **Stock decaf coffee (and regular).** By the time dessert rolls around, some guests will surely be a bit drowsy. Others, however, will be in a cold sweat wondering if the hummus was made in a facility that processes tree nuts. Stock regular and decaf so everyone wins, regardless of cortisol load.

9. **Forgive your guests' poor behavior.** For some people, one too many glasses of wine will lead to a bit too personal a rendition of "Let It Go"; me, I'm going to fuck up your candles. Please don't look at my shame.

10. **Know when to say goodnight.** The surest way to spoil an otherwise delightful evening is for guests to overstay their welcome. You served a delicious meal, regaled your company with your adventures in Peru, and then there was the time you were chased by a wild boar in Tuscany. You laughed. They cried. But now you need to take off your pants and briefly entertain the idea of doing the dishes before abandoning it and then refusing to floss. If your guests seem to be settling in for a hard winter, clearing the table, yawning, and talking about your early start in the morning should give the hint that it is time to leave. If they are obstinate, firing up your CPAP machine will do the trick.

Those are the basics. There are of course other things you should consider, such as the right balance of guests (men to women, singles to couples, physical trainers to holes in the head), guests' allergies, and having a spare bed in case anyone really enjoys that single malt, but those topics were less important than sharing my desire to utterly destroy your candles. I regret nothing. **B**

MICHAEL THORNTON *lives in Cambridge, England, where he is currently writing a book on cocktails and entertaining. He is a Deputy Editor of this magazine.*

BY JAY RUTTENBERG

ABOUT OUR "C"...

Anybody can have an off-night

There it is, displayed in the window for all to see, our own Scarlet Letter: the Department of Health's ignominious "C." We want to take this opportunity to explain its origins to you, our customer. We take *great pride* in our hygienic standards, and do not want decades of an almost fanatical commitment to cleanliness to be eclipsed by what amounts to one off-night.

During our most recent health inspection, our point total was severely diminished because a diner brought her aged and rheumy Korthals Griffon into the restaurant, hiding the dog beneath her table. Obviously, we were unaware of the dog's presence, and were completely blindsided when the health inspector discovered it, chewing on a bloodied rat while fending off the attacks of a second hound — a flea-infested snarling stray that, we later discovered, had trailed the Griffon into the restaurant in order to mate.

It goes without saying that the Department of Health did not look kindly upon this incident. There was egg on our face — we mean that literally: When the inspector proceeded to the kitchen, he discovered our sous chef, a Moe Howard partisan, covered in egg custard pie — which, to our chagrin, had gone rancid. Might the sous chef's indiscretion been ignored, had he been wearing pants? We shall never know. But we do take solace in the fact that our saucier apparently has impeccable aim, even on the nights she is inebriated to the point of vomiting.

Had the violations ended there, we would have been awarded a solid "B." Not ideal, but manageable. Unfortunately, on the night of the inspection, even well-intended health measures backfired. For instance, it was determined that a roast was being kept at a legally acceptable temperature. But the inspector priggishly took issue with the fact that earlier that evening, the kitchen's meat thermometer had been rectally employed by a busboy, checking whether his flu was severe enough to warrant missing his shift. (RIP Eddie, 1989–2016.) And in the men's room, our eccentric-but-beloved attendant Sergio had replaced the traditional "Employees Must Wash Hands" notice with an impassioned handwritten diatribe explaining how such instructions are a conspiracy of the soap industry. Where we saw an opportunity to engage in dialogue about Big Cleansing, the health inspector simply saw a bathroom without soap. (The inspector, it must be said, was a bald-faced germophobe, making a great show of covering his mouth when he coughed.)

While we assume full responsibility for our "C," we strongly disagree with certain criticisms. Take our chef's drooling. Is it really the place of the health inspector — a cisgender, American-born male — to impose his personal biases on our chef's cooking methods without considering the cultural mores of his homeland, Cincinnati? And in regards to our famous lobster bisque, did the inspector find toxic levels of chalk? Of course. But let's be reasonable. This is New York City, 2016! How is a restaurant expected to woo clientele without a phalanx of sidewalk chalkboard easels filled with witty coffee puns and beautifully rendered phalli?

Finally, there was the issue with the waitstaff. Let's put aside any salacious hearsay and concentrate on the facts: When the health inspector discovered "the jar," we made a mistake — really, our only one of the evening. Did our management present the inspector with the restaurant's comeliest waiter and waitress, offering a no-tell chance to have sex with one of them, right there on the sauté station? Yes. And it was wrong. *But was it attempted bribery?* According to our lawyer — a highly paid professional with an impressive advanced degree — it was not. And while it was perfectly within the inspector's rights to refuse our offer, the absurd, unseemly vehemence with which he rejected it suggests that a profoundly sex-negative agenda has crept into the Department of Health and Mental Hygiene. *We believe this must stop.* If you agree, please sign our petition at Change.org. You can win a chance for a free Thanksgiving dinner.

We feel confident that future inspections will yield more satisfying results. And certain longstanding problems — the faulty urinal partitions, the maître d's fingernails — have already been addressed. In any case, we appreciate your patronage, and thank you again for dining at Per Se. **B**

MIKE REDDY

JAY RUTTENBERG

is editor of **The Lowbrow Reader** *and of its book,* **The Lowbrow Reader Reader** *(Drag City). His work has appeared in* **The New York Times**, **newyorker.com**, *and* **Mad**.

Comics

Merrill Markoe

My discontent with the show was by no means the fault of The Beatles. I do not hold them personally responsible for **THEIR ASSHOLE FANS!!**

THE DIARY OF MERRILL MARKOE: ACTUAL EXCERPTS

8/19/64   When Denni and I arrived at the Cow Palace and were confronted by a troupe of girls carrying British flags, I knew we were in for trouble. But when The Beatles came out, the screaming was so bad it was TORTURE!! I had to put my hands over my ears!

The truth was we never did get to hear The Beatles right through the whole show. And after thinking what a vast disappointment and waste of money the whole thing was, I was quite depressed.

The only thing I heard Paul say was "THANK YA VERA MOOCH."

I was so bitter that when a man asked me how I enjoyed the show, **I BLEW UP AT HIM!**

B

Tales of the QUICKSAND KID
by Howard Cruse

QUICKSAND!! WHEN I WAS A KID DOWN SOUTH, I WAS **OBSESSED** WITH THE STUFF!

CAN I STAY AND SEE IT **TWICE**?

AS LONG AS YOU KEEP BUYING **POPCORN**.

ANYTIME A **JUNGLE MOVIE** WOULD COME TO OUR LOCAL **PICTURE SHOW**, I'D BE **FIRST IN LINE** AT THE **BOX OFFICE**.

PEOPLE IN JUNGLE MOVIES WERE **ALWAYS** GETTING STUCK IN QUICKSAND!

AGAIN?

HELP, **TARZAN!!** SAVE ME!

I COULDN'T GET **ENOUGH** OF THOSE SCENES!

ONE OF MY CABINMATES AT **SUMMER CAMP** TOLD ME THERE WAS SOME **QUICKSAND** IN HIS HOME TOWN OF **CHUNCHULA.***

NO KIDDING?!

*SEEMS **UNLIKELY** IN RETROSPECT, BUT AT THE TIME I WAS TOTALLY **THRILLED**.

I DROVE MY FOLKS **NUTS** THE NEXT TIME MY FAMILY WENT ON A **VACATION**.

PLEASE CAN WE GO THROUGH CHUNCHULA? PLE·E·E·EEEEZE??

FORGET IT! THAT'S AN **HOUR** OUT OF OUR **WAY**!

I'M NOT SURE **WHAT** I IMAGINED I WOULD **SEE** DURING A QUICK SWING THROUGH CHUNCHULA....

OBOY!

...SOMEBODY BEING SUCKED OUT OF SIGHT NEXT TO THE **DAIRY QUEEN**?

HELP!!

WE DIDN'T **HAVE** ANY **JUNGLES** NEAR WHERE I LIVED IN ALABAMA, BUT WE DID HAVE LOTS OF **WOODS**.

WOODS LOOKED A **LITTLE** LIKE JUNGLES IF YOU **SQUINTED**.

WHAT I WOULD HAVE DONE IF I HAD ACTUALLY **SPOTTED** SOME QUICKSAND IN THE WOODS IS AN **OPEN QUESTION**.

OH, **WOW!** LOOK **THERE!**

I DEFINITELY WOULDN'T HAVE WADED **INTO** IT UNLESS I HAD A **FRIEND** STANDING NEARBY WHO COULD PULL ME **OUT**.

NOW **DON'T** GRAB ME UNTIL I **TELL** YOU TO.

OK.

I WASN'T **CRAZY**, JUST **CURIOUS!**

ONE TIME I DISCOVERED A PUDDLE OF **GOOEY MUD** BESIDE A **DRAINAGE CULVERT**.

MY PAL MARCUS KEPT A **RESCUE BRANCH** WITHIN EASY REACH OF ME WHILE I **STOOD** IN IT TO SEE IF I'D START **SINKING**.

NOTHING YET....

THERE WAS AN EPISODE OF THE OLD "LASSIE" TELEVISION SHOW FROM THE 1950s THAT HAD QUICKSAND IN IT.

Woof!

OH, WOW!!

TOMMY RETTIG PLAYED JEFF MILLER, A KID WHOSE FAMILY LIVED IN A RURAL FARMHOUSE THAT SEEMED A LOT LIKE FARM-HOUSES THAT MY FRIENDS IN GRAMMAR SCHOOL LIVED IN.

MOM

GRAMPS

LASSIE

JEFF

IN THIS EPISODE, JEFF, LASSIE, AND JEFF'S FRIEND PORKY WERE EXPLORING SOME WOODS NEAR JEFF'S HOUSE AND PORKY STUMBLED RIGHT INTO (YOU GUESSED IT) A POOL OF QUICKSAND.

woop

OOPS.

JEFF COULDN'T REACH HIM, SO IT WAS OBVIOUSLY UP TO LASSIE TO SAVE THE DAY.

GO GET HELP, GIRL!

I'M SINKING! I'M SINKING!

AGAIN?

Pant pant pant pant pant pant pant

?? WHAT ARE YOU TRYIN' TO TELL US, LASSIE?

Woof! Bark! Arf!

Y'SAY PORKY IS STUCK IN QUICKSAND?

S'GONNA TAKE A HEAP O' SCRUBBIN' TO GET THOSE DUDS CLEAN, SON.

PORKY WAS RESCUED, OF COURSE...

BUT BOY! WAS THAT EXCITING!

THEN THERE WAS THE KID'S NOVEL I CHECKED OUT OF THE COUNTY BOOKMOBILE ONE TIME IN WHICH SOME GIRL WAS WALKING ACROSS A PRAIRIE AND SHE PASSED A COW THAT WAS UP TO ITS SHOULDERS IN QUICKSAND.

OH, DEAR.

MMM·GLUB*

*"HELP!!!" IN COW LANGUAGE.

THERE WAS NOTHING SHE COULD DO ON HER OWN...

OH, DEAR, OH, DEAR...

...OH DEAR!!!

...AND THERE WERE NO GROWN-UPS ANYWHERE NEARBY TO HELP.

SO SHE WALKED ON BY AND LEFT THE POOR ANIMAL TO FEND FOR ITSELF.

Guilt

LATER THAT DAY SHE TOOK THE SAME ROUTE **HOME**.

Dread...

THE **QUICK-SAND** WAS STILL THERE...

~Gulp!~

...BUT THERE WAS NO SIGN OF THE **COW**.

THIS **ATE** AT ME FOR **DAYS!** I COULDN'T STOP THINKING ABOUT HOW THE COW MUST HAVE **FELT** ONCE IT COULDN'T GET ANY MORE **AIR!**

AT NIGHT I STARTED HAVING **NIGHTMARES** ABOUT BEING **TRAPPED** LIKE THAT COW.

HEL-L-LP! LASSIE, **SAVE** ME-E-EE...

I FORMULATED DESPERATE **SURVIVAL STRATEGIES** IN MY **SLEEP.**

EVEN AFTER MY **HEAD** HAD GONE UNDER, MY PLAN WAS TO **HOLD** MY **BREATH** AND KEEP REACHING AS **FAR** ABOVE THE **SURFACE** AS I COULD IN HOPES THAT **SOMEBODY** WOULD **NOTICE** IT FLAILING AT THEM AND PULL ME TO **SAFETY.**

MAYBE **JESUS**, EVEN...?

RELAX, FELLA. I'VE GOTCHA.

I'VE GOTTEN **CALMER** ABOUT THESE THINGS BY **NOW**, BEING AN **ADULT** WHO'S SEEN **YOU-TUBE VIDEOS** THAT DEMONSTRATE HOW YOU CAN GET YOURSELF OUT OF QUICKSAND PRETTY **EASILY.**

HEY, I COULD DO **THAT!**

FOR SURE, I STILL HAVE MY SHARE OF **NIGHTMARES**, BUT THEY TEND TO BE ABOUT TRAUMAS THAT ARE **CLOSER** TO MY **EVERYDAY LIFE.**

HELP!! SOMEBODY **SAVE** ME! I'M GOING BANK-RUPT!!

BE CAREFUL WHERE YOU **STEP** THERE, JOEY. THAT STUFF'S **DANGEROUS**

HELP!

THE OCCASIONAL PASSING ENCOUNTER WITH **QUICKSAND**, I CAN TAKE IN **STRIDE.**

CRUSE ©2016

The End

JOHN WILCOCK IN:

The story behind Larry Adler, FLEXIDISCS, AND ECHO:

"The Magazine You PLAY on Your PHONOGRAPH"

In JANUARY 1958, Harmonica wizard LARRY ADLER returned briefly from London to play a gig at THE VILLAGE GATE...

Adler had left America some time before, after being incorrectly maligned as a Communist for his collaboration with Paul Draper, a TAP DANCER.

I DECIDED TO DEVOTE A COLUMN TO ADLER. *I wanted to know* why so many people played harmonica, and as a novelty sound. Yet in his hands it produced such WONDERFUL music. He told me:

One of the drawbacks of harmonica is that it's almost TOO EASY to play.

I could TEACH somebody in fifteen minutes. But then they might play all of their lives and never put any of THEMSELVES into it.

I LOVED ADLER'S POIGNANT & EVOCATIVE MUSIC. Teamed with pianist ELLIS LARKINS, Larry produced some stylish Gershwin...

Larry seemed perfect for a new project with which I was getting involved...

You see, SEVERAL YEARS OF OFFBEAT COLUMNS HAD GIVEN ME A REPUTATION FOR THE BIZARRE ... So it was fitting that I was approached by Barrie Beere, a wealthy entrepreneur, who came to me with an idea:

JOHN! I got me a HOT TIP!

I mean **HOT!** Okay: I love magazines, AS YOU KNOW. Well! ... *My GIRL* ... she just *returnee vooh'd* from PARIS with one'a the *weirdest ones* I've ever SEEN!! The pages were RECORDS you could BEND, JUST LIKE PAPER!

Barrie was referring to the **flexi-disc!** ... The first modern instance being a mail-in giveaway for Nestlé Chocolate, in 1957. (JUST SEND IN THREE WRAPPERS!)

(John's role in ECHO was as Editor & Creative Director) The idea for ECHO, influenced by France's SONORAMA, was to combine articles with overlapped flexidisc audio.

CENTER-CUT HOLE FOR PLAYER

SIX FLEXIDISCS PER 32-PAGE ISSUE

SPIRAL BINDING

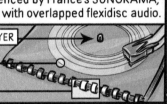

ECHO's format was so unconventional in the U.S., that its application for 2nd Class Postage prompted a LENGTHY discussion from Post Office Examiner William A. Duval:

" The ISSUE is whether the publication is formed ENTIRELY of printed sheets. I have concerns with this for significant reasons:

Yes, the publication is COMPOSED in part of printed sheets, BUT it is NOT composed ENTIRELY of printed sheets. Now, I am not an AUTHORITY in the publishing business, but looking at this publication there are five SO-CALLED "sheets" in it which are of rather heavy stock paper or cardboard and it APPEARS that the musical record that COMPRISES this sheet has been IMPRESSED in some manner other than printing UPON this particular type of sheet.

How is this record, then, a PRINTED SHEET!?

One other thing that might be POINTED OUT is that these pages or sheets on which these phonographic records appear are susceptible of being REMOVED from the publication. There is no indication that that is what is INTENDED to be done with it because the instructions as to how to play these records indicate that the publication is opened to the record that it is desired to play and the remainder of the publication is folded UNDERNEATH it so that the desired record appears on the top. The publication is THEN put on the turntable of the phonograph, and the needle placed MANUALLY in the grooves that appear on the surface so that it APPEARS that it was intended that the pages remain within the binding; and it is entirely POSSIBLE, it appears on the surface, that the publication be used in accordance with the instructions for its use that appear in the publication. NONETHELESS, on the basis of the findings I conclude that as a matter of law:

Application for 2nd Class privilege is DENIED!"

DID YOU KNOW?

Seemingly as "U.S.A. as It Gets" ... The Flexi-Disc was FIRST invented by the Reds! ... As Russian *SAMIZDAT!*

Discarded X-RAYS were cut into CIRCLES and then etched with transcription equipment to distribute BANNED MUSIC.

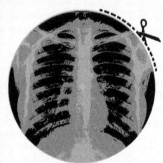

They called these discs ROENTGENIZDAT! which translates to:

"X-RAY pressed RECORDS!"

— now available at your local morgue —

The Post Office decision was a BIG financial blow. Especially as we'd already SPENT *quite* a lot of dough...

... We had already converted a rehearsal tape of songwriter JULE STYNE with (hello!) GYPSY ROSE LEE ...

... Induced artist JULES FEIFFER to illustrate routines by comedians MIKE NICHOLS & ELAINE MAY ...

... And picked up the sounds of FRED ASTAIRE dancing, with an interview by NAT HENTOFF ...

...Finally, we even rehabilitated

Larry Adler

Scorned and hounded out of the country by Joseph McCarthy, Adler offhandedly mentioned JAMES THURBER was a friend. Off I went to Thurber to ask if he'd write a lauditory piece to accompany Adler's music.

Sadly, Echo was before its time... And despite many other GREAT PAGES, including audio of EDWARD MULHARE with SALVADOR DALI, ECHO folded after just four issues.

x

More strips online at http://www.ep.tc/wilcock

THE KIDS MOVIE

BY David Chelsea

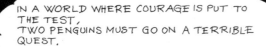

IN A WORLD WHERE COURAGE IS PUT TO THE TEST, TWO PENGUINS MUST GO ON A TERRIBLE QUEST.

NO, I WON'T GO TO SLEEP, AND I WON'T EAT MY MUSH... TILL YOU TELL HOW WE TURNED INTO RABBITS--

YOU HUSH!

WE STOPPED THEM LAST YEAR, BUT WILL THEY EVER LEARN? FIND OUT IN "THE SUGAR CUBE ROBOTS RETURN"!

WHAT A CREEPY, DECREPIT VICTORIAN HOUSE!

NOT AT ALL LIKE THE CONDO WE RENTED IN TAOS.

HIDDEN UNDER THE STAIRS THERE'S THIS DUSTY OLD NOOK, AND WITHIN IT WE FOUND A MYSTERIOUS BOOK.

THERE'S A PORTAL UPSTAIRS TO DIMENSIONS UNKNOWN. MOM AND DAD STEPPED INSIDE. NOW WE'RE ALL ON OUR OWN.

I'VE GONE ON THE WEB AND DECIPHERED THE RHYME-- TO SAVE MOM AND DAD WE MUST GO BACK IN TIME!

IT'S A DANGEROUS QUEST, AND YOU CAN'T COME ALONG.

THAT'S SO SEXIST! I'LL SHOW YOU THAT GIRLS CAN BE STRONG!

THE VALLEY OF MINGE IS DIVIDED BETWEEN A MALEVOLENT WITCH AND A COLD-HEARTED QUEEN.

IRONIC Fashion ROLE MODELS

WHEN YOU WERE YOUNGER, IRONY PROVIDED YOU WITH THAT MUCH-NEEDED "OLD-BEYOND-YOUR-YEARS" LOOK...

"PIONEERS"

"CAMP GLAMOR"

"TORTURED GOTH"

"DUSTBOWL REFUGEE"

TODAY YOU WANT TO BE YOUNG AT HEART, BUT YOU REALLY LOOK LIKE...

A GRANT WOOD PAINTING

DAME EDNA

A FAT VAMPIRE

A CRAZY HOMELESS WOMAN

INSTEAD, CONSIDER THESE TRIED-AND-TRUE, BONA FIDE, AGING HIPSTER ROLE MODELS!

COLETTE

MARIANNE FAITHFULL

SCARE SMALL CHILDREN!

SCARE YOUNG ROCKSTARS!

WILLIAM BURROUGHS

KEITH RICHARDS

SCARE GROWN MEN!

SCARE EVERYONE!

B

Zen of Nimbus
by Michael Sloan

The Doozies
by Tom Gammill

Brush Up Your Insults

S	C	H	I	S	M		T	A	P		S	L	O	G
T	R	E	M	O	R		I	C	E		C	I	A	O
B	E	E	F	W	I	T	T	E	D		I	N	F	O
E	T	D			A	U	D	I	T	S				
D	A	E	D	A	L	U	S		C	A	S	U	A	L
E	N	D	U	R	E			A	T	O	N	C	E	
		B	E	S	L	U	B	B	E	R	I	N	G	
A	B	S		E	P	A			X	E	S			
T	R	I	P	E	V	I	S	A	G	E	D			
M	A	L	A	W	I		P	R	I	C	E	S		
S	T	O	N	E	S		C	H	A	N	G	E	U	P
	C	R	I	M	E	A			N	G	O			
T	I	A	A		B	E	D	P	R	E	S	S	E	R
A	M	O	K		L	I	E		A	M	O	U	N	T
J	O	K	E		Y	R	S		P	U	L	S	E	S

© 2016

A Beach Ball.

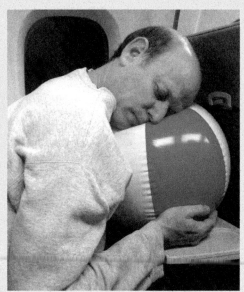

To Joey Green, it's a airplane pillow.

Gone are the days of complimentary in-flight champagne and cushy sleeping-car coaches on the Orient Express. Say hello to $50 "legroom upgrades" and bedbug-infested hotels. What's a weary traveler to do?

Hang tight—it's Joey Green to the rescue! *Last-Minute Travel Secrets* contains tons of ingenious travel tips that may sound quirky at first but really do work. You'll discover how to overcome obstacles using common household products, like how to . . .

- Sneak liquor aboard a cruise ship with food coloring
- Wash your clothes with a salad spinner
- Cook hot dogs in a coffee maker
- Seal hotel curtains with a clothes hanger
- And much, much more!

Last-Minute
TRAVEL
SECRETS
JOEY GREEN
121 INGENIOUS TIPS
TO ENDURE CRAMPED PLANES, CAR TROUBLE, AWFUL HOTELS, AND OTHER TRIPS FROM HELL

CHICAGO REVIEW PRESS

www.joeygreen.com

B

INDEX TO THIS ISSUE

Afghanistan section, EPCOT Centre, failure of, 21

Agoraphobia, Davy Crockett's, 93

Amistad, in 3-D, possibility of, 87

Answers, Spot the Difference Quiz, 45-48

"I'm drunk," 45

"I'm not wearing pants," 46

"My yarmulke is striped," 47

"Stain on kimono is Juicy Juice, not blood," 48

"Hold on, that is blood," 48

Astrophysicists knowing secrets to universe, but not knowing about *Army Man* magazine, tragedy of, 154

"Bagel and lox spreads at exorcisms," a poem, 130

Bailey, Beetle 821

Sex tape 822-45

Bible, midgets in, 2

"Biker beards on urologists," photo gallery, 83

Bikram yoga smells, best to worst, 71

Blasting doo-wop to impress Millennials, effectiveness of, 1

Blues Brothers, The, 419-476

Comedy locked in briefcase the whole time, 421

Rubber biscuit choking myth, 420

Boner contests, amateur, 189

Boner contests, professional, 190

C+C Music Factory, shuttered by Better Business Bureau, 449

Captain Jack, will he get you high tonight or not?, 263

Carrying around samurai sword at Disney World, advantages of, 19

Cheers, 41-237

"Coach Gets A Diaper," lost episode, 42-44

Cheerleaders of indoor football league, dating possibility even for comedy writers?, 107

Chicken Soup for the Impotent, xxx-xxxi

C.K., Louis, fetishization of scalp freckles, 71

Clowns who emerge from out of deserts, holding bloody knives, 53

Cock rings from Zales, 68

Cohen, Leonard, 548–587

Disco musical, failure of, 557

Former member of Harlem Globetrotters, 587

Opens for ELO, 562

"So Long, Marianne" when used as wedding line-dance, 581

Competitive eaters, 56–87

Not in habit of using cloth napkins, 60

Complete Idiot's Guide to Home Amputation, The, 87

Conflict Resolution the Pol Pot Way, lxiv

Crystal, Billy, 22-41

Hair color, 25

One-man show, "Night of 1000 Negro Jazz Guys," 35

Problematic impersonations of, 40

Psychosexual rivalry with Joe Piscopo of, 23

Underground kickboxing career of, 27

Cube, gleaming of, 24

Dahmer, Jeffrey, 726

and gluten allergies, 726

podcast potential of, 726

Trumpet player for Blood, Sweat & Tears, 726

Definitive Oral History of Being Sick of Oral Histories, the oral history, 51

Dentists offices that blast Norwegian death metal, 375

Diarrheaara, British spelling of, 40

Epipens, 14-27

Use of as currency in Montessori schools, 78,

Velvet Underground songs glamorizing abuse of, 41

Epiphanies experienced in handicapped stalls of strip clubs, 130

Escobar, Pablo, favorite sitcom *Veronica's Closet*, 12

Fields, W.C., least known quote: "The problem with me is that I always think with my heart. And my cock. And my wallet. And my brain. Mostly my brain. And my wallet. Sometimes my cock," 21

Flavor Flav's Illustrated Kama Sutra, ccc

Ford, Gerald, hottest state-funeral hook-ups, 42-59

Friends 543-546

Abandoned Spin-offs, 547

Chandler the Clown, 547

Gunther's Fat Farm, 547

Hell Pit Apocalypse, 547

Hi, I'm Gary, The New Friend, 547

I Will Hunt You Down, 547

Submarine Secrets, 547

Gigolos named Wally, 18

God Is Great! (But Can He Help Me with My Horrific Gas?), lxxxii

Goonies rumors, 207–415

Based on 1956 John Updike novel, 298

Kids played by trained orangutans on knees, 411

Original ending involving Supreme Court trial, 412

Shot entirely in basement of Prince's Paisley Park estate, 412

Sloth not love Chunk after all; Sloth love his own self, 414

Gottfried, Gilbert, sexy dreams involving, 255

Guys named Glen, notable, 6

Hasidic astronauts, lack of, 55

Hasidic gay icons, lack of, 56

Hasidic zombies, lack of, 56

Human Centipede 3: The Novelization, an excerpt, 381 - 390

Human thumbs, resemblance to Dwayne "The Rock" Johnson, 98

Humor pet peeves, 55–82

Hot-air balloons crashing into KKK picnics, 58

"I Don't Get Drunk, I Get Awesome" yarmulkes, 124

Ikea, perfect place to dispose of body, 77

Ikea sex swings, 28

The Pleasure Syndicate *is Mike Sacks, Ted Travelstead, Scott Jacobsen, and Todd Levin.*

Hiring experts to install, 28
Warranty details, 28
Inch-long cocaine fingernail on brain surgeons, 6
Jammin' on the funk, 8
Jared the Goblin King wig from *Labyrinth*, 80
Joe Dirt 2: Glamorous Hollywood Premiere Party, photo display, 89 - 94
Jokes, how to properly tell, 45–48
   In funny ethnic Asian accent, 47
   Lying on ground, on back, legs well spread, 47
   While hopping, 46
   While winking, 48
   Yelling at top of lungs into bullhorn at a riot, 48
   Yodeling from artificial hills, 47
King, B.B., 67
   Cowell, Simon, advice to dress more provocatively, 67
   Cowell, Simon, advice to lose a little weight, 67
   Cowell, Simon, advice to not be so sad, 67
   Lucille: Lesbian?, 67
Knievel, Evel, spy for Israel, 76
Keurig home coffee machine, popularity among Hell's Angels, 90
LaRouche, Lyndon, cabaret act of, 89
"Lil Miss Hairy Pussy," 1940s syndicated comic strip, 101
List of only 25 people in world not associated in any way with comedy, 34
Little Rascals, 3-98
   "All were actually adults" theory, 3-6
   "Cranky Spanky" muffin-throwing incident, 77
   Urban legend involving Darla and Pete the Pup, 89
Little, Rich, 113
   Little Richard feud, 113
Losing your virginity, worst places, 108-112
   Back of Hallmark Store, clutching "Precious Moments" figurine, 111
   Bathroom on Greyhound, en route to Dollywood, 109
   Dressing room, Montgomery Mall's Forever 21, 674
   Four cars back at Rockville, Maryland, Hardee's drive-through, 108

   "Personal Grooming Aisle," Dollar Store, 111
   Sandals Resort, Bahamas, strapped into rented parasail, 112
   Scientology Center, hooked to e-meter, beneath oil painting of L. Ron wearing a jaunty sailor's cap, 112
   Spirit Air shuttle, La Guardia, 112
LOVEBLACKCOCK, popularity of Wi-Fi name, 378
Love, Mike, 87
   Really cool hats, 87
   Writing one word on *Pet Sounds*, 87
Michaels, Lorne, sexualized depictions of in Japanese manga, 67
Mike + the Mechanics, band that went down with RMS Titanic, 37
Mimes 77 – 87
   Can they speak?, 77-78
   Invisible box real?, 79
   Never experience good weather in mime world?, 85
Miscavige, David, 236-282
   High-fiving the pope, 280
   Kind, patient religious figure, 236
   Lute playing, 245
   That really swish look when wearing kick-ass shades, 240
   Wiseness of, 248
   Xenu, sexual relationship with, 277
Mistakenly sneezing "Allahu Akbar!" while on airplanes, 43
Mr. Holland's Opus, deaf child, annoying, 86
Nicknaming testicles "Brenda and "Eddie," 38
Nipple rings from Kay's, 69
NPR fan fiction involving Terry Gross getting banged from behind by a two-headed dragon, 288-313
Nude Fran Lebowitz, eating sushi off of, 85
Performing puppet shows at fraternity parties, 4
Pink camouflage tactical gear, use of by ISIS, 50
Pinkie out while masturbating, appeal to women, 571
Piscopo, Joe, imitating Bruce Springsteen, historical importance of, 24
Pope, all-time favorite Three Stooge, 2
Prostitutes nicknamed after domestic cars, 851

D. WATSON

Prudhomme, Chef Paul, drunken scooter race, 90

Puppetry of the penis, as violation of Geneva Convention, 173

Purple Crocs, when worn to your own murder trial, 51

Putin, Vladimir, childhood acting career of, 21

Raccoon blood stains on rented white tuxes, 298

Richie Rich, cartoon character, rumors of being rich prick, 78

Scat music, Constitutional ban of, 49

Seducing Women With a Little Guile, a Positive Attitude, and $1,000,000 in Cash, 9

Seltzer water, discovery on Mars, 6

Seven Habits of Highly Successful Dock Whores, x–xv

Sex is Like Pizza Because… 18–25
    Always delivered to house by a teenager or foreigner in thirty minutes or less, 21

    Always goes a little better with coke, 20

    You need napkins, 24

Something about the Beatles, 221 - 987

Stride, break-a my, ain't nothin' gonna, 56

Tap dancers, 221-6, 241
    Convicted of arson, 221
    Famous, 241
    Favorite cheeses of, 224-6

Tapeworm Diet, The, xvii-xviii

Threesomes: two fucking, one watching reruns of *Mr. Show*, 92

Twists, M. Night Shyamalan, least popular, 45-98
    Aliens are afraid of kosher wine, 76
    It was the hermit crabs, 47
    Monsters hate their eggs scrambled, 81
    Script was never completed, 62
    Time machines don't take diesel, 87
    Wood sprites are incapable of growing very large afros, 78

"Ugly Monkey with Sweet Tooth Who Fall from Sky and Cause Mayhem," working title for *E.T.*, 31

Urinating, dreaming about, 43

Vampire poetry, unpublished, 87-781

Vasectomy scars that look just like sad emoticons, 96

Voyager, the three songs on board, 61
    Bach's Cello Suite, 61
    Mozart's Requiem, 61
    "This is How We Do It" on cassingle, 61

"Why Your Affliction Bothers Me," a children's tale, 227

Worst magazines to see in your shrink's office, 329-345
    Big Black Hairy Cocks, 333
    Don Diva, 345
    Girls 'n' Corpses, 344
    Marvelous Titties, 329
    National Review, 330

Wrigley Field hot dog vendors, sexual predilections of, 60

BY MATT MATERA & ALAN GOLDBERG

Brush Up Your Insults

In case of emergency, check page 87

ACROSS

1. Breaking point
7. "Big Bottom" band, for short
10. What solving this puzzle isn't, hopefully
14. Moving experience?
15. When dry, it emits steam
16. "Kisses!"
17. *"Shit for brains" (*Troilus and Cressida*)
19. Poop
20. When you're going (abbr.)
21. Taxing experiences?
23. Architect of the Minotaur's Labyrinth
27. One way to keep a sexual relationship
31. Put up with
32. Now and not later
33. *"Mouth-breathing, blithering" (*Henry IV, Part I*)
37. Six-pack components
40. Org. established in the same year as the Clean Air Act
41. Marks, crudely
42. *"Butt-ugly" (*Henry IV, Part II*)
49. Southeast African nation and lake
50. They may be high in Amsterdam tourist areas
54. Fab Four alternative
55. Switcheroo
57. "___ River" (Justin Timberlake mondegreen)
59. Give Directly or Oxfam, *e.g.*
60. ___-CREF
63. *"Shamu" (*Henry IV, Part I*)
67. Dangerous way to run
68. "This answer is in Esperanto," for example
69. Total
70. One is: "Why do seagulls fly over the sea? Because if they flew over the bay then they'd be bagels."
71. There's 100 in a cent.
72. Throbs

DOWN

1. Venerable English religious figure (abbr.)
2. Minotaur, for example
3. Obeyed
4. Ethan Hunt's org.
5. Piggy miss
6. Test that might diagnose an ACL tear
7. "___ Andronicus" (more Bardly content!)
8. Destroyed, as a test
9. What to take to a nail salon?
10. Cut from a magazine
11. ___-Manuel Miranda (*Hamilton* genius)
12. Lout
13. Nickelodeon slime, for example
18. Greek letter used as a Christian symbol by Franciscans
22. Modern name in London?
24. Nickname
25. "___ we having fun yet?" (*Party Down* catchphrase)
26. __ Brown and His Band of Renown
28. Operating system born at Bell Labs
29. Teenage (bad) dream?
30. Stocking stuffers?
34. Word often punned upon in Hawaii
35. Brown co.
36. Sheepish sound
37. Cheddar producers (abbr.)
38. A spoiled one can give you indigestion
39. Granary
43. Dessert for a pipe-playing god of nature?
44. Large jug
45. Not clandestinely
46. Academic mean, for short
47. Sea eagle
48. Burrow down or eat up
51. The next American one is in 2020
52. Levy of *Best in Show*
53. Calvinball and 43-Man Squamish
55. Gives up
56. "More direful ___ betide that hated wretch, / That makes us wretched by the death of thee" (*Richard III*)
58. Former Israeli leader Golda
60. First name of a Mughal empress's last place
61. Internet TLA disclaimer
62. Right as rain
64. Genre for two *Hamilton* Cabinet battles
65. Big bird
66. Local star

CPSIA information can be obtained
at www.ICGtesting.com
Printed in the USA
LVOW06s0335071116

511241LV00004B/6/P

9 780692 799550